THE ANATOMY OF THE
KINGDOM
And
THE POWER OF
COMMUNITY

Exchanging Religion For A Life of Function and Purpose

ALSO BY ANDREW E. GUY

Work Your Words:
Finding Your Pathway To Personal Success

A book on personal development and how to empower others to achieve their dreams. This is a must read for anyone who wants to grow and improve his/her personal life for greater success.

THE ANATOMY OF THE
KINGDOM
And
THE POWER OF
COMMUNITY

Exchanging Religion For A Life of Function and Purpose

ANDREW E. GUY

An Imprint of GladshareMediaPublishers

Copyright © 2016 by Andrew E. Guy

THE ANATOMY OF THE KINGDOM AND THE POWER OF COMMUNITY:
Exchanging Religion for a Life of Function and Purpose

All rights reserved. No part of this book may be reproduced or transmitted in any form or by any means without written permission from the author. Unless otherwise identified, Scriptures and quotations are from the New International Version of the Bible (NIV), © 1973, 1978, 1984 by the International Bible Society. Used by permission of Zondervan. All rights reserved.

ISBN 13: 978-1987890006
ISBN 10: 1987890000
Printed in the United States of America

Gladshare Media Publishing
www.gladsharemedia.com

DEDICATION

To the billions created in the image of God whose greatest desire is to have a relationship with the King but have settled for a conduit in the form of religion that has alienated them from the original glory that was promised before the foundation of the earth. May you uncover your identity, and discover your destiny as you function with divine purpose.

To every youth who has ever wondered if God was too BIG to relate to their little problems. I hope that as you discover God's great purpose for your life you will become a replica of the kingdom in motion and a *LIGHT* in your community.

To every church *"who"* is not a building and to every building that is not a church, may you discover the *"real church"* and cultivate a community where people and relationships take precedence over religious mindsets.

To every pastor and leader, may you discover the gifts inside your community and commit this to memory: *Leadership is crucial but wise counsel save lives.*

To every seeker, may you look within before you venture out into deep space, because your Creator never left...He's closer than you think.

ACKNOWLEDGEMENT

Most worthwhile efforts contain elements of progress, sacrifice and tenacity. The completion of this assignment was no different. The elements listed not only reflect my role as the author, but also describe the direct and sometimes indirect participation of several other people whose contributions I not only applaud but also honor.

To my beloved wife, Theresa, who selflessly walks with me through thick and thin. Your remarkable insights have been transforming. I love you.

To my two handsome "Dudes", Therand and Alin. Your unconditional love and support inspire me to function *optimally* as "Daddy".

To my mentor, the late Dr. Myles E. Munroe (1954 – 2014) of Nassau, Bahamas. You are a legendary ambassador of the kingdom of God and, in my opinion, a great gift to humanity. Your in-depth and experience-based teaching led to a paradigm shift for me and thousands of your "students" on our perspective of Religion versus the Kingdom of God.

To my dear mother, Una Guy, you are a true testament for mothers of the 21st century and beyond.

To my adopted "Daddy", the late Rupert Samuel Blackwood (1942 - 2014). You provided a foundation that I could firmly build my life upon. And to Deanne Fields Goldman (Mamma DEE) and Mr. Gary S. Glover (CW5 US Army - Ret.) Thank you all for exemplifying the kingdom in motion in the most practical ways.

The assignment of presenting a spiritual concept within the framework of scientific facts would have been a daunting task if it were not for two teachers in my life (noted below) who truly utilized their gifts to impart knowledge with awe-inspiring passion and skill.

To my Biology professors, Dr. Henry Robison and the late Dr. Hugh H. Johnson, of Southern Arkansas University, Magnolia Arkansas. Because of you two, the complexities of Biology were unraveled in a way that simplified the structure and function of living organisms and made science a useful part of life. And in true character of great teachers, I have become a life-long learner of the study of life science.

To God almighty, the ultimate designer and creator of all things seen and unseen – from you alone, one became many and the many became specialists with gifts to maintain homeostasis in a "community-body" that reflects the kingdom of God in motion.

CONTENTS

	ACKNOWLEDGEMENT	*viii*
	PROLOGUE:	*xiv*
	(The world as a body)	
	INTRODUCTION	18

PART I: **THE ANATOMY OF THE KINGDOM**

Chapter 1.	Structure Meets Function	27
Chapter 2.	The Kingdom And The Body Defined	37
Chapter 3.	Kingdom Culture And The Body systems	55
Chapter 4.	Knowing Your Gift Makes Way	69

PART II: **THE POWER OF COMMUNITY:**
                   THE KINGDOM IN MOTION

Chapter 5.	The Power of Community	81
Chapter 6.	Together We Win	91
Chapter 7.	Misconception of "Service"	105
Chapter 8.	Community Meets A Need	121

PART III: **MAKING COMMUNITY WORK:**
                    CONNECTION IS KEY

Chapter 9.	The Technology Analogy	139
Chapter 10.	Kingdom Connectivity	153

...CONTENTS

PART IV: **EXCHANGING RELIGION FOR A LIFE OF FUNCTION & PURPOSE**

Chapter 11.	The "R" WORD That Rules The WORLD	169
Chapter 12.	The Path To Truth	182
Chapter 13.	In Pursuit of Authenticity	192
Chapter 14.	Dynamic Participants	200
	Epilogue	222
	Kingdom Prayer of Liberation	226
	Training and development	228
	Call To Action	230

THE ANATOMY OF THE
KINGDOM
And
THE POWER OF
COMMUNITY

PROLOGUE

Every day is a journey toward destiny. And as we begin our journey through these pages, I would like us to start by asking ourselves a question. One of which I believe, aside from spiritual wellness, to be life's crucial and most intriguing question that will lay the foundation to help us discover purpose, understand how to maximize our potential, live a life with meaning and fulfillment, and function holistically with optimal precision in the community where we live, work, play and pray:

If the world were an interconnected body made up of diverse organs, which organ would you be, and what is your function?

PROLOGUE

I want you to think about that for a minute or two and then briefly look at the picture on the next page—the world as a body. It is perfectly okay if you are not able to answer this question right now, or even after you've completed your analysis of the diagram. The main purpose of this warm-up exercise is to get you to start thinking about your function and how you fit into the big picture of God's plan for your life.

PROLOGUE

THE WORLD AS A BODY

Briefly look at the picture below to see if you can find yourself as an organ, and then discover your function:

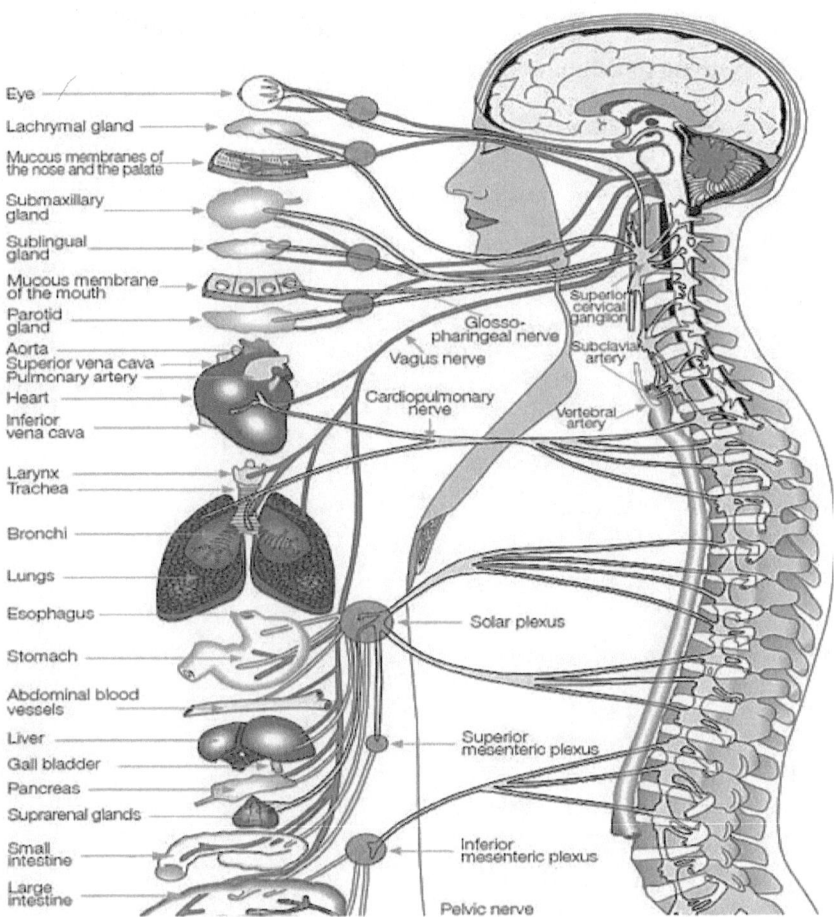

Fig. 1. Harvard-wm.org

NOTES

The World As A Body

[Fig. 1]

1. McPeek, Emily. "Human Anatomy in Harvard-wm.org." *Human Anatomy in Harvardwmorg*. HUMAN ANATOMY IN HARVARD-WM.ORG. Web. 19 May 2015. main-human-body-systems-and-thei-connection.jpg

INTRODUCTION

SCIENCE PROVIDES BOTH A THEORETICAL and a practical framework for the study of the human body. More specifically it is the branch of Biology that opens the window into the intricate details of how the human body is made up and how it works. This aspect of Biology is known as Anatomy (structure or makeup) and Physiology (function or the way something works).

The Holy Bible, comprising Old and New Testament, provides the spiritual framework for the study of Jehovah God and the function of his kingdom. And more specifically, many scriptures in the sixty-six books of the Bible provide masterful details that reflect the Anatomy and Physiology of the Kingdom of God.

Many people would protest any association between Science and the Kingdom. But a close examination of the latter through the eyes of Anatomy and Physiology undeniably demonstrates that the human body has an intentional and elaborate design that can no longer be limited to the interpretation of Science alone.

We are a part of a much bigger picture. One that involves bringing God's kingdom to earth. One that binds mankind to his

Creator. One that demands unity among humanity. One that leads to purposeful living beyond a job description.

THE SEARCH IS ON

The Kingdom of God is like a human body, with millions of complex structures, functions and assembled components designed to work together as one big unit. They both have a structure, a function and a purpose for their existence. However, while the structure (anatomy) of a person, place or thing embodies a specific function (physiology), purpose reigns supreme in the grand scheme of all creation.

Because of this, an intense search in pursuit of purpose has now ensued and humanity has devoted its entire livelihood just to make sense of the reason we are all here on this third rock called Earth. This monumental, centuries-long search has led the world system to become a broken record, replaying pre-historic traditions, which has unfortunately become the go-to music for modern times. And it permeates two major areas of society namely, science and religion.

There is a growing population of the world that relies solely on the academic contributions of science to shape their daily lives or reveal the purpose and meaning for it. And even though millions of dollars are continually endowed to this field, most of it really is to assist the world in understanding theories that apply to our general existence. Hence, the quest for purpose and meaning in an individual's life do not provide enough significance to warrant the disproportionate allocation of resources to such a pursuit. Therefore, the search for purpose continues to be an internal operation.

Introduction

Comparatively, religion attracts a far greater audience when answers to life's purpose and meaning are sought. For centuries, religion with its myriad of segmented labels has been woven deeply into the tapestry of many communities worldwide. It is an institution devised by humankind with a general objective of establishing oneness among its followers through specific instructions on the meaning and purpose of life.

Unfortunately, it appears that religion has only served to repel humanity so far from ourselves that it will take *"Pluton years"* to bring us back together. Like the blast of an atomic bomb that separates particles for hundreds of miles, our distances have driven a wedge into our very souls that have not only impaired our vision but have also created a mass separation for generations.

This vast distance has reduced humanity to mere finger pointing, name-calling and objects of malfunction without purpose. Sadly, even Christianity, with its focus on love for God and others, has fallen into this *attitude*—having a label without a function. Leading many followers to *"...having only a form of godliness but denying its power"* (2 Timothy 3:5a).

THE RIGHT BOOK FOR OUR TIME

So, "Where do we go from here?" you ask. Where do we find the answers to the meaning of life and the purpose for living? This book, *The Anatomy of the Kingdom and the Power of Community*, was written for this reason.

Firstly, the writer takes the stance that since Jehovah God is the Creator of mankind and the universe, we should look to Him for answers concerning the purpose and meaning of life.

Introduction

Secondly, this book establishes that life is a gift that has been given to us for a purpose. Now within this life, the process of living embodies diverse components which validate the gift of life. Through the process of living we utilize our gifts to demonstrate that we have talents, skills and abilities that not only need to be unveiled but just as importantly they also need to be valued.

Thirdly, *The Anatomy of the Kingdom* is a revolutionary book that will help you bridge the gap between function, purpose and meaning. It will assist you in discovering how your area of giftedness fits into the big picture of living. You will come away with a much clearer understanding of the power of community and how our interconnectedness improves efficiency, builds unity, promotes balance and inspires hope. You will be inspired to appreciate the value of your own talents, skills and abilities as well as those around you.

You will be empowered to seek and embrace effective relationships instead of a religion. You will begin to live a fulfilled life; one that is purpose-driven and choice-led as you serve others in your community where you live, work, play and pray. You will be encouraged to become a person of influence and efficiency in your community.

GOD'S INTENTIONAL DESIGN

Like the human body, you are members and part of a complex system of specialized cells, tissues and organs. These are interconnected and assembled in communities to function as one unit in order to create, support, build and maintain an internal balance known as homeostasis. In this book you will

Introduction

discover that your anatomy and physiology are no accidents. They are a supernatural "blueprint" designed as a true replica of God's "***kingdom in motion***." You will discover practical truths that will set you free from *doctrinal* mediocrity and catapult you to a life of function and true purpose.

My hope is for you and millions like you to come to a revelatory knowledge that everything about you was designed to emulate the kingdom of ***"God in motion"*** as you function with supernatural purpose to create meaning in every area of your life.

My desire as we journey through these pages together is that you will find your reason for living, your calling for service and your passion for getting up every morning. Like oxygen to your body's (somatic) cells, discovering your purpose will be the breath of life that keeps you getting up again and again. Remember, *purpose adds value to your life and function validates the life you live.*

"There is one body and one Spirit, just as also you were called in one hope of your calling; one Lord, one faith, one baptism, one God and Father of all who is over all and through all and in all."
~Ephesians: 4:4-7

PART- I

THE ANATOMY OF THE KINGDOM
"A Replica In Motion"

The Kingdom is a supernaturally governed operation that has a spiritual function with a physical manifestation in the form of your anatomy and physiology through the serving of one's gift in a community. You are an instrument for greatness and an incubator of God's presence.
~*Andrew E. Guy*

CHAPTER 1

STRUCTURE MEETS FUNCTION
"The Anatomy & Physiology of the Kingdom"

The interconnected world around us is comprised of many structures and functions that give rise to a vastly complex system that supports life on earth. To aid our understanding of anatomy and physiology, and to demystify life in general terms, we will examine the role of science in society.

The field of science has played a significant role in enabling us to bridge the gap between the association of structure and function. Science is both a tool and an interlinked field of study with many branches having diverse specialties. As a tool, science is not a replacement for the spiritual aspects of humanity; however, it helps us to understand the physical world we live in.

As a general overview and precursor to our discussion, it is important to note that the field of science is made up of four main categories also known as *L.A.P.S.* sciences (life, applied, physical and social) sciences. Within these broad categories are many sub-branches of diverse disciplines.

Life Science is the study of life and living organisms. Applied Science is the discipline of converting scientific theory into practical applications. Physical Science is mostly concerned with naturally occurring objects, properties of matter and energy and has four sub branches I call S.P.E.C (*Space, Physics, Earth, and Chemistry*). Lastly, Social Science is primarily concerned with relationships. How people relate to each other and the study of humane society. This behavioral science of relating is the foundation of all communities.

ESTABLISHING PROTOCOL

Our focus for this book will be on the branch of Life Science and its integration with Social Science, and specifically, Human Anatomy and Physiology, which is the study of the human body and its interconnected functions. Biology, for example, is a branch of science that deals predominantly with the study of life. Anatomy is the study of the internal and external structures of the human body parts and their interdependent relationships. Physiology, on the other hand is the study of how these functions affect the internal environment of living things and the sequence of events that occur at the chemical and molecular level.

Both anatomy and physiology are complements of each other. Anatomy elicits the mentioning of physiology the same way that structure involves the functioning of specific organs and the role they play in a shared interdependent environment. The body is made up of trillions of small structures called cells. Specific cells then come together to form tissues and organs, and groups of organs assemble to form a much larger system known as an organ system. These organ systems further assemble to make up an interactively interdependent and more complex system called an organism.

To help you get the most from this book, it is vital that you have at least a basic understanding of anatomy and physiology. In the most simplistic terms, think structure when it comes to anatomy (*the what and where*); subsequently, think function when it comes to physiology (*the how and why things happen the way they do*) in a living system like the human body. It is my intent to show how the design of the human body is similar to the kingdom of God in both structure and function.

I have been involved in the study of science for many years, with particular emphasis on movement and structure and how they influence the human body from a biological and physiological perspective. Over this period, I have had the privilege to serve as a science teacher, a 2nd Dan (degree) martial arts instructor, fitness instructor, rehab therapist, earned degrees in Human Biology and Exercise Science, a master's of science in Kinesiology and Human Performance and destined to complete my doctorate in the near future. Still, I am completely amazed each time I think about the human body with its intricate design and infinite functions.

I will say that with all the earthly knowledge and finite wisdom we glean from the great minds of the past, present and future, we will never come close to the proximity of the intellect of God, his self-sufficiency and his magnificent power.

Among his infinite creations, humankind takes precedence. We are his masterpiece, a spiritually encapsulated work of art that brings him great pleasure. *"For we are God's handiwork, created in Christ Jesus to do good works, which God prepared in advance for us to do"* (Ephesians 2:10). We are his workmanship, designed to reveal his purpose on earth and to make the supernatural kingdom a practical experience for everyone. Together we are a *kingdom in motion* that brings him glory. As a community we jointly make it possible for the kingdom of God to become the reality that our biblical ancestors of faith could only envision.

In addition to biblical scriptures, the field of science has provided only a window of opportunity for humanity to have a glimpse into the mind of its Creator. There have, however, been many who have made significant discoveries and progress toward understanding the abundance and mysterious wonders of God's creation. Among them are Aristotle, known as the earthly crowned father of Biology; Herophilus of Alexandria and Andreas Vesalius, both hailed as fathers of Anatomy along with Herman Boerhaave and Claude Bernard who many respectably refer to as the fathers of Physiology.

Indeed, the field of science has had its share of great discoveries and technological innovations that will continue to make advances for the betterment of humanity for years to come. And so, it is within this framework that God's divine plan for humanity will be explored.

OVERVIEW OF A KINGDOM

By definition, a kingdom is any realm (country, region, state or territory) that is ruled by a king or queen. Those of us who were born in the last few decades have only a limited exposure to the concept of kingdoms because they have now evolved significantly into modern forms of government.

Today, there are almost as many variations in the approach to governance as there are letters in the alphabet to the tenth power and perhaps even more. Some of these include absolute monarch, anarchy, communism, democracy and totalitarianism.

Kingdoms of old were established by certain principles and expanded mainly as a result of winning a territorial war, obtaining an inheritance, by marriage gift or in more rare occasions, being elected to a ruling position of king or queen. The fame of a kingdom was determined by its size. The more land or domain a king or queen possessed, the more powerful their kingdom was considered to be.

Kingdoms existed as a derivative of the ruler's subjectivity. Because of this, the nature of kingdoms reflected a vast diversity of personalities. However, despite the variations of sovereign leadership styles, all kingdoms have core fundamental components that determine their existence. Among these are:

- Power------------(Source/influence/ability)
- Head--------------(Cephalic/superior part of a structure)
- Body--------------(Soma/Mass: collection of working parts)
- Structure----------(Components/Anatomical make-up)
- Function----------(Process/Responsibility)

- Purpose------------(Mandate/Assignment)
- Community------(Environment/Culture/Atmosphere)

Power: A source with the ability to do work that will influence change. In reference to kingdoms, the sovereign ruler is the source of power. It is the ruler who determines how this power will be utilized. A kingdom is only as powerful as its ability to demonstrate a function to create lasting change that permanently affects the constituencies it rules.

Head: Cephalic, (Greek, *kephalikós)* means pertaining to the head or referencing the superior most part of any structure. In ancient kingdoms, the head is referred to as the king, queen, emperor, empress or other sovereign designation. In most cases, headship was absolute and no external input from other sources was allowed.

Body: Soma, (Greek, *sôma)* referring to the body or a collection of mass or working parts that make up a whole unit. The body of a kingdom is the supporting components, its people or citizens who carry out the assignments and the subjective will of the king, queen or sovereignty.

Structure: A conduit, a form or anatomical makeup of a body, place or thing that is derived as a result of its internal components. Kingdoms also have these structural components, king/queen, council, advisors, army and citizenry. All of which serve as a support to maintain the king's domain.

Function: The responsibility or collaborative process by which work is done to maintain influence. All function is based on the blueprint of an original design that governs a series of sequences to accomplish the intended purpose for which the structure was made. In other words, function is synonymous with purpose and it is the end result that reveals the mind of the creator. In a kingdom, function is the demonstrated process of how the will of the sovereign will be carried out.

Purpose: The mandated assignment given to any structure that must be accomplished to reveal the mind of the creator. Therefore, the purpose of every product is to validate the creator's intention with such precision that it glorifies the creator's decision for making the product. Function validates purpose and purpose reveals glory, and glory identifies a created process. In a kingdom, purpose is the will of the king.

Community: An atmosphere or specific environment created by the choice-led relationships of like-minded components that function as specialized structures to sustain each other to create homeostasis. All citizens comprise the community of a kingdom, and their interactions reflect the will of their ruler, while meeting a core need of social interaction. The community of a kingdom is enlarged through the acquisition of territories. The larger the territory the greater the domain and the influence of the sovereign.

ELEMENTS OF THE KINGDOM OF GOD

Just as there are earthly kingdoms, there is also a heavenly kingdom. Earthly kingdoms are physical and therefore visible. But the Kingdom of God is spiritual and therefore invisible but his power is manifested through his creation. *"But we have this treasure in earthen vessels, so that the surpassing greatness of the power will be of God and not from ourselves..." (2 Cor. 4:7a KJV).*

Despite the significant difference between the two realms, the basic elements of earthly kingdoms are the same as those of the Kingdom of God. It is important to note that God's kingdom was in place long before the establishment of any earthly kingdom or realm and it will continue to exist well beyond them as well. Each element listed below, therefore reflects that God's time-span for the reign of his Kingdom is from everlasting to everlasting.

In God's kingdom, Jehovah God is the source of all **power**. He is the all-powerful one, possessing the ability to do all things. (Psalms 62:11). *"One thing God has spoken, two things I have heard: Power belongs to you, God..."*

Although God the father is the source of all power, he chose to confer **headship** over all creation to his son Jesus (the) Christ. On two separate occasions Jesus acknowledged the following:

Luke 22:29, *"And I confer on you a kingdom, just as my Father conferred one on me..."*

Matthew 28:18 *"Then Jesus came to them and said, "All authority (power) in heaven and on earth has been given to me."*

So it was as the head of the kingdom that Jesus issued the assignment for his followers to *"Go and make disciples of all nations..."* (Matthew 28:19a). These first followers had become kingdom ***citizens*** who made up the earthly population of ambassadors. Their assignment, as well as ours is to bring the culture of heaven to earth and thereby expand the kingdom of God.

The structure of God's kingdom is very unique. It is the only kingdom in which the entire population of citizens are part of the royal family who serve as kings. In Luke 22:29, Jesus "***conferred***" the kingdom on his disciples. Also in Revelations 5:10, "*You have made them to be a kingdom and priests to serve our God, and they will reign on the earth.*"

In the kingdom of God function and purpose work together to manifest his glory. Ephesians 4:16 states that "*From him the whole body, joined and held together by every supporting ligament grows and builds itself up in love, as each part does its work.*"

It is only when we function in God's kingdom to manifest his glory that we validate his divine purpose to form *community* and to intentionally expand the kingdom on earth. "*The kingdom of heaven is like yeast that a woman took and mixed into about sixty pounds of flour until it worked all through the dough.*" (Matthew 13:33). In other words, the culture of the kingdom functions like yeast. It is the function of the Holy Spirit that works through us "*To will and to do his good pleasure*" until we become saturated with the mind of God, as we manifest the will of God and go throughout the world to make more disciples until the entire earth is filled with the kingdom mind-set and the glory of God.

THINKING IS FOR THE *BRAIN* BUT DREAMING IS FOR THE *MIND*…ONE WEIGHS 3 POUNDS, THE OTHER IS *INFINITE*.
~*Andrew E. Guy*

CHAPTER 2

THE KINGDOM AND THE BODY DEFINED
"A Replica In Motion"

The Anatomy of the kingdom is God's mandate in motion for establishing the kingdom culture of heaven in the earth. It is a community-centered function with divine purpose and not a religious practice. In the similitude of the human body (anatomy and physiology), the kingdom is a completely organized system (a community) of members with specialized functions that establish, promote, support, and maintain an internal balance (homeostasis) that brings credibility, glory and honor to the original creator of all things—God. It is only through this function that the *kingdom in motion* is made possible.

Conversely, the Kingdom of God is not a religion; it is a government and a living system of functions based entirely on divine service to the body through intentional relationships. Kingdom is synonymous with relationships and order. This order is analogous to the internal functioning of the human body, otherwise known as homeostasis, when the internal environment is free of chaos and at a state of balance. It is at this state that optimal functioning is established and purpose discovered. Like the body, you are part of a collection of specialized members that assemble to reflect a kingdom in motion. Everything about you has the structure and function of a kingdom that represents motion, order and diversity.

From science and technology to motion picture and still photography, the imprint of the kingdom is embedded in your genetic make-up, DNA (Deoxyribonucleic acids) from the beginning of time. Although the human body is highly complex in its design, each segment jointly works together as one unit to produce and maintain life.

Now ask yourself, what is this *"Kingdom"* that we speak of? Is it a system of merely classifying plants and animals into groups based on their specific functions and characteristics? Or more specifically, is it the six-tiered nomenclature system of taxonomy based on the scientific Swedish genius, Carl Von Linnaeus (botanist, physician, zoologist, and author of the groundbreaking book, *Systema Naturae*, Leiden, 1735), that revolutionized the world of science from the 17th century onwards? No, not by a longshot—the kingdom we speak of is the Kingdom of God whose divine purpose is only activated when we become kingdom citizens.

The kingdom of God is the government for reproducing God's mandate in the earth. It is God's blueprint for effective living and every citizen of the kingdom has **the freedom to function with a divine purpose through the effective use of your giftedness to influence and transform the world.** This Kingdom is beyond anything that the earthly realm can even think or imagine, because it can only exist inside of you through the presence of the Holy Spirit of God.

Now what would you say if I told you that you see, feel, hear, and interact with God's Kingdom every day of your life? And even more surprising, what if I told you that everywhere you go you carry around the Kingdom of God with you? That it is active and alive in us. While you are sleeping, walking, talking and even doing nothing, so it seems, the Kingdom is with you. The Kingdom is not a religion, neither is it some mystical fairytale that exists only in some faraway galaxy.

Because the kingdom is a system of function that governs the will of God, it is important to note that even though we are all God's creation and have the structure of his kingdom within us, not all of us function with purpose. True purpose and function comes from being connected to the source of God through the Holy Spirit. (See chpt. 10. *Connection is key*). A body without the spirit has no function, so is having the components of a function but lack the connection to perform. It is the spirit of God that connects with our human spirit and guides us to all truth.

Therefore, *God's Kingdom is a supernaturally governed operation that has a spiritual function with a physical manifestation in the form of your anatomy and physiology through the serving of one's gift in a shared community.*

In other words, the Kingdom of God is a function that is based on intentional relationships and its sole purpose is to establish, display and make known in the earth and to all inhabitants, the likeness of God, the ultimate King and Creator of all things seen and unseen, present, past and future. When you think of the kingdom, think of systems of relationships within a body called a community. Because the Holy Spirit is the direct connection to the kingdom, the community could be anywhere you live, work, play, and pray. It is not subject to occupation, location or educational aptitude. The kingdom concept is a blueprint designed with the Creator's divine purpose as its focal point, you.

"Neither shall they say, See here! or, see there! for, behold, the kingdom of God is within you." (Luke 17:21 *AKJV*) Do not look to your left or right, in essence, the Kingdom of God is inside of you; and not only that—you are the kingdom in motion and everything about you is a direct replica (model and representation) of the kingdom of God in motion in the earth realm. Your body (the temple) is a representation of the complete function and purpose of how the Kingdom should operate on earth.

Since the earth is diversely populated with over seven billion people, with various backgrounds, tongues, skin tones and eye colors, together we jointly make this planet a place called home. In fact, when God made the earth, his original intent was that everyone would be a part of his kingdom. (The story of Adam and Eve in Genesis tells why that did not work). Everyone has all the necessary components but there must be a connection to the source through the Holy Spirit.

Adam had direct connection but lost the government (the function of the kingdom) when God's Spirit left the earth. It is the work of Jesus Christ through the Holy Spirit which reconnected mankind back to God. The components (man's anatomy and physiology) that were once without function and purpose now have a divine destiny through faith in Christ.

But why would a king die for a bunch of fallen "*Adamites?*" This is the part where most people get stuck and ask themselves: *Why me? What did I do to deserve this? I'm no body special?* But if they only knew that the answer they seek is simple but quite profound. God, the Creator and giver of life has placed a gift inside of you (in the form of a function) that can only be used through the connection of his spirit to manifest his glory on earth.

This is what it means to have life abundantly: to do more than just exist but to live and possess the gift of life in all its abundance without lack; to have more than you'll ever need so you spend every waking day giving your gift away to make the world a better place. And the best part is that serving becomes the reward that fills you up, adds meaning to your life and purpose to your living. Can anyone do this? Absolutely! Do you have to be a preacher or some religious figure? Absolutely not! Just come as you are.

Unlike religion (more on this later) the kingdom of God is not concerned about your title or external appearance (the container or wrapper that holds the gift); however, it is entirely focused on the gift (the content) that is inside of you. Everyone is gifted differently and so the gifts were given to various individuals to function as one unit. But without the right connection to the source (*just like a computer to a server or an engine to a battery*), even the most gifted will become useless.

Therefore, any structure that does not have the appropriate connection will cease to function correctly and therefore abort purpose. In essence, you could have all the components but lack function if you are not connected.

THE ORIGINAL INTENT

The original intent of the Creator was that everyone created in his likeness would be a part of his kingdom by virtue of function and purpose. Function, means using the gifts he gave them to serve and to fulfill the ultimate purpose of establishing, maintaining and replicating his presence in the earth.

Now, it will take every person, every gift, every talent and every level of skill implanted into mankind to accomplish the monumental task of the kingdom. The kingdom needs everyone because every person was designed to be included in the Creator's plan. I call it the ultimate diversity and inclusion plan. Every gift plays a vital role in the kingdom. Matthew 18:12, the parable of the lost sheep paints the perfect picture. I believe Jesus told this story to show the value of every person in the kingdom.

The shepherd was willing to leave the ninety-nine sheep to save just one lost sheep. Ever wondered why? Because there is a possibility that the ONE had everything that the NINETY-NINE lacked and who knows what critical function could be trapped inside of the *ONE*. Likewise, if a builder designs a house but lacked the one skilled trade (the roofer) to complete the project, the house is only a figment of his imagination and will never become a reality.

"It takes every kinda people to make what's life about," said singer and songwriter, Robert Palmer. And I could not agree more. From the street sweeper to the CEO, and *"across*

the board" all the way to Presidents and Prime Ministers, the Kingdom is for everyone. For there is but *"One God and Father of all, who is over all and through all and in all."* (Ephesians 4:6) This means that God is at the very core of your being, from the atomic level and beyond because his blueprint for life is trapped inside of you and your purpose for living is to translate this blueprint into a function that brings him glory.

STRUCTURED FOR ONENESS

The structure of the Kingdom of God is present in all of God's creation. If you were created in his image and in the power of his likeness, you are a part of a system of specialized components who serve a divine purpose in the body of your community. As we journey through this book, I will show you how the role you play in your community adds value to everyone and why communities collapse due to lack of citizen participation and exclusion from shared resources.

Keep in mind that our example for this discussion is the human body, which has been a part of you from day one. The unique design of your anatomy levels the playing field for every human. No one is greater or lesser or more significant than another; we all share a common design that is supernaturally beyond the mental scope of humanity. However, the creator has made it possible for us to have a relationship with him through the work of Christ and the reconnection of the Holy Spirit to Creator. He has also given us a commonality that binds all of humanity together.

We are not different levels of human speciation (a subunit or branch) we are, however, God's creation. We may have different appearances, but we are designed to function as a unit, one big family under the sun. Instead of coming together and functioning as one cohesive unit, some have chosen isolation and as a result, malfunction because all the components are no longer operating as a unit. Instead of one kingdom, one God, one mission, one purpose and one faith, we have many gods, many isms and religions (Atheism, Catholic, Christianity, Islam, Scientology, and the list goes on). And *"If a kingdom is divided against itself, that kingdom cannot stand"* (Mark 3:24).

Remember, we all have the potential and structure (anatomy and physiology) to function, but some are susceptible to failure because they lack connection to the source. Still, there are many in the kingdom today who are without function because they misunderstand the purpose of their gift. If you do not know your purpose for living you will misuse your gift. Therefore, your knowledge of who you are comes from knowing the purpose for why you were created. And this is made known through the spiritual connection of the Holy Spirit who reveals the wisdom of God in our hearts.

Now, everyone has all the necessary vital components (heart, lungs, kidneys, musculature, nervous, skeletal, and organ systems) to maintain life in the body. In the same way, each of us are like cells, tissues or organ systems in the body that have a uniquely specialized gift to serve others in our chosen communities where we live, work, play, and pray. And since the kingdom is about a system of specialized structures and functions (the anatomy and physiology) with one purpose, each member must do his/her part for the overall success of the system. ***As specialized organs in a shared interconnected environment, we are the sum total of the atmosphere we create.*** Therefore, our every action grossly affects the environment we live in and every other component within that shared space.

If one fails, the other suffers. Think of it this way: What do you think would happen if you had a heart failure? Do you think that your cardiovascular accident (heart attack) would have a drastic effect on your ability to live? Yes, it would. The same is true in the kingdom of God. Everyone plays a vitally interdependent role in God's grand design. One for ALL, and ALL for the good of ONE to the glory of God.

FUNCTION GIVES MEANING

The anatomy and physiology, the structure and function of your body, gives meaning to your life and purpose for living. Every member must interconnect and lend support for the good of all. We each have what the other person needs. We are more than our brother's keeper; we are the lifespan of those we connect with in communities. Therefore, no individual is one hundred percent furnished but each of us is specifically designed to complete someone. This is why we must serve our gifts. In the field of science we call this *specificity*. It means to be peculiar, not general, singular, not broad. There is a gift that you have that no one else has; there is skill that only you can do that cannot be replicated. You are the only original.

The cardiovascular system is incomplete without a heart to pump oxygen and nutrients to the working body cells; as a result, the body will become impaired and die from the starvation of oxygen and malnutrition. Just like the human body, we are interconnected with those in our shared space or community and our survival is interdependent. In simple terms, ***I need you and you need me and we need them and the world needs us***.

Another way of helping you to wrap your mind around this concept of God's kingdom in motion is for you to identify yourself as an organ within the human body. Think of the body as your chosen community and you are an organ inside that community who plays a vital role in maintaining life for everyone. Since every person is either a cell, tissue or an organ in the body of a community, let's assume you are the brain in your community with a specific function and people are body cells. Plus, let us also assume that everyone knows the purpose and function of the brain as described below.

Neuro is short for nerve or nervous system, while neuron is a specialized cell that transmits electrical messages and *Neuroscience* is an applied discipline and a branch of science that studies how the brain works. Among other organs of the body, your brain is very powerful. The basic principle of neuroscience is the understanding of the brain's functions and the various anatomical structures that make thinking possible.

The brain is by far one of the most powerfully revered organs in the body; yet it only weighs a little more than three pounds, but it is not the most important among living things. Even though you are the brain and *one* of the most powerful body organs, your power comes from a combination of subparts that make you *one united structure*.

STRUCTURE MEETS FUNCTION

> *"I need you and you need me and we need them
> and the world needs us"*

Remember, each of us is part of a whole that comes together to create an intricately complex system that works as one unit. Identical to the anatomy of the kingdom of God, the brain has several subunits that assemble to form a unit of thinking parts within the community of the nervous system. Neuroanatomists know that these brain parts play a vital role in your overall functioning, especially since you are the brain for this demonstration.

Although it is not common practice for the average human to go around using the anatomical scientific names as part of their daily vocabulary, I suppose by this time you are probably wondering what are the subparts that make *"you"* as the brain so powerful among other body organs.

Here are some of the major parts that make up your unit:
- *Amydala*
- *Anterior cingulate cortex (ACC)*
- *Basal ganglion*
- *Pre-frontal cortex*
- *Cortex*
- *Corpus callosum*
- *Hippocampus*

These are not listed in any particular order and are only included to aid your understanding and to get you familiarized with the vocabulary terms. Without these specialized components, the brain would cease to be a functioning unit. All these subunits make the brain the powerful instrument it is. Together each part completes the brain and makes it one of the most used organs in the human body.

Take for example, the *cortex*. This region allows you to interact with your environment then recall and reflect on those experiences at a later point in time. The *corpus callosum* bridges the gap and connects the left and right regions of the brain called *hemispheres*. Without this *special bridge*, the right and left sides of your body would not be able to communicate. The left controls the right side of the body, while the right *hemisphere* controls the left side of your body. Every human has two *hemispheres*.

The *pre-frontal cortex* of your brain allows you to multitask and do many things at once. It helps you with planning and goal setting. The *Amydala* is the emotional center of the brain, while the *basal ganglion* is your reward center that deals primarily with motivation and inner drive to perform repetitive and rehearsed activities like walking, running, standing, bending etc.

Even though we have only listed a few structures, there are many other components in the brain that jointly make it function efficiently, and the kingdom of God is identical. Every one of us is vital to the overall success of the body of Christ. We, like *glia cells* of the brain consistently carry out specialized functions for the good of those who are connected to us. And since we are all part of the same environment, our interdependency is the key to our survival.

Now that you have improved your basic knowledge of the brain and a few of its many functions, imagine the brain without a *corpus callosum*. Who would bridge the gap to connect both sides of the body? Or, how would you make plans without the *pre-frontal cortex,* and how would you experience and interact with your environment and other people? As a brain in the body, you play an extremely essential role in the complete functioning of every process. We, therefore, as body cells could not live without you; in fact, our entire livelihood depends on you. As you function, thank you for *"thinking"* about us down here—the *body cells*, your next-door neighbors.

Finally, imagine the body without a brain—inconceivable! The same concept applies to the kingdom of God. You are God's gift to me and I am God's gift to you; together we are instrumental gifts to the world. We have a great work to do and the completion of our function, purpose and destiny makes us a very necessary part of God's plan.

A SYSTEM OF FUNCTIONS

From our discussion on the brain, we discovered that the kingdom of God has both a structure and a function with a divine purpose. In this section, we will see how the body, like the kingdom, has a specific design that includes everyone. In other words, the kingdom has a makeup or structure (anatomy) and a function (physiology) just like the human body, where each part is assembled to form a *community-body* of the kingdom and perform specific functions as a service to each other based on the individual's gift to represent God's kingdom on earth.

The term *"God's kingdom on earth"* means a state of balance (homeostasis) with access to unlimited resources and an atmosphere that brings glory, honor and credit to the Creator as collected groups of people use their gifts to serve each other. Everyone in the community benefits when each member functions and does its part. More specifically, each joint supplies the other and lends support to maintain homeostasis in the entire body.

In the same way that the human body is composed of trillions of small cells, and these cells *aggregate* (come together) to form tissues, specific tissues with like functions join to make larger members of the body called organs. Groups of organs, then assemble to make the organism call a body. Each body receives a lifespan, a function in the form of a gift and a purpose to fulfill. You may call it life's BIG assignment if you will. But in order for each organism to fulfill its created purpose, it must function in a community by utilizing its gifts to serve others.

To help you grasp the concept of the kingdom, your basic understanding of the anatomical human body is paramount. Although we will not go into great depth, the basics will do for this discussion. The kingdom of God is like a body with members that function interdependently and connect to serve each other to maintain a stable environment known as homeostasis. Homeostasis then, is a state of balance, or a condition where the body is in complete harmony within itself and its environment. This means, it has a specific temperature that allows it to function optimally.

According to scientists, 98.6 degrees Fahrenheit is the ideal temperature for optimal body function. Any fluctuation above or below this ideal temperature is viewed as an imbalance and causes the body to change. Some of these changes are necessary adjustments made to bring the body back into a state of balance.

Like people in a community, organs function to serve each other for the overall good of the body. And because everything in the body is interconnected, any sudden change in one organ affects the other. I am a firm believer in the power of fitting examples to declutter life's terrains. For that reason, I will try to help you make the necessary connections as we journey along by providing you with as many examples as possible.

For instance, pretend you lived in a cold climate and there was a sudden drop in your body temperature. The body may go into shock and you would feel very cold. Because of this unexpected drop in temperature, your body will respond by shivering as your muscles rapidly contract in order to generate more heat to warm the body. In the same way that these internal responses happened automatically, you may instinctively rush for a blanket or increase your layers of clothing to insulate your body against the cold temperature.

This state of chill is called *hypothermia;* meaning, (not enough heat), where the body is unable to maintain optimal body temperature and plunges into a state of panic. Your brain interprets this condition as a stressor, thus releasing a stress hormone that causes the body to transition into fight or flight. If you were to take a closer look at your skin you would notice tiny pimples or *goose bumps*, as the *arrector pili muscles* (tiny muscles attached to hair follicles) of body block the pores to provide insulation and retain body heat.

The opposite is also true when your body temperature fluctuates far above one hundred degrees Fahrenheit ($100^0 \, F$), you would experience a condition known as *hyperthermia* (over heating) or excess thermal conduction of the body's internal environment. Unlike *hypo*thermia where the body tries to retain heat, *hyper*thermia is the reverse. The main objective is to release as much heat as possible and bring the body temperature back down to normal.

The adverse effects of *hyper*thermia to the body are similar to when an egg is fried. Denature, warping or distortion of protein cell structure occurs when an egg undergoes severely high temperatures. Similar effects are experienced with *hyper*thermia, including high possibilities of neurological brain damage. And because the skin is the *largest organ* in the human body, sweating is the ideal regulating process for removing heat (cools the body) through evaporation.

Aside from cooling, sweating provides other benefits to the body, such as removing toxins and excess salt, but our main purpose here is to demonstrate what happens when either system is triggered in extreme conditions. There are many other systems responsible for regulating body temperature, but your brain's *hypothalamus* (a structure in the brain) and sweat glands are essential.

It is also important to note that neither of these two extremes is conducive to homeostasis and optimal functioning of the body's internal operation. In either case, *hypothermia or hyperthermia*, the body makes the necessary adjustments to maintain normalcy. Now how does body temperature helps us to understand community? Just like body cells, each person serves as a regulator in his community the same way the body's thermostat regulates temperature to maintain homeostasis. Each joint supports the other so that everyone will be completely furnished.

> If you don't know where you are going,
> Every road will get you nowhere."
> ~*HENRY KISSINGER*

CHAPTER 3

KINGDOM CULTURE AND THE BODY SYSTEMS
"None Greater Than The Other"

The kingdom of God has a culture that is similar to the systems of the human body. As we journey through this book together, my hope is for you and others to gain some basic knowledge of how your body functions in relation to that of an interconnected community of people. Let's dig a little deeper.

Every kingdom citizen is part of a system that makes the body of Christ functional, all are important and no one part is more important than another is. This means, no part of the body, or people, for that matter, whether large or small, inside or outside, above or below, none is worthless or considered vestigial (of no functional use) as some scientists will lead you to believe.

Even though scientists do not know everything there is to know about the human body, a significant amount of scientific research has led to mankind having a greater understanding of themselves. Science does play a major role. Through scientific revelations *(which I completely believe is a gift from God and His attempt to reveal himself to humankind)*, we understand that the body is a unit, a multicellular living entity consisting of trillions of smaller subunits called cells.

While some cells may perform vital functions such as the heart and brain, no one cell is considered greater than another; although, some cells combine to make up larger tissues and organs, which perform extremely vital functions to maintain life in the body. Actually, I cannot think of any part of the human body that is insignificant or vestigial—meaning, having no known functional benefit to the body.

Among other body structures, scientists suggest that the *spleen*, the *coccyx*, (the human tailbone) and the *appendix*, (a narrow tube that dangles off the colon) are vestigial and have no seemingly useful function in the human body and are therefore dispensable.

AN ARGUMENT TO CONSIDER

Could some of the scientific decisions being made today grossly affect our future? What if the cells we discard today are the lifejackets of tomorrow? Scientist could be half-right, or they could also be utterly wrong. Take for example, some biological functions, like hormones and specialized enzymes, many of which are only active under specific conditions.

The thymus gland, for instance is extremely vital during the developmental stages of children. It was once thought that this enlarged structure was harmful to developing children and should be discarded because "the thymus gland does not participate in the control of the immune response." [1] Some even believed that "the thymus had become vestigial during evolution and was just a graveyard for dying lymphocytes" [2] In addition, it was also concluded that "the presence of lymphocytes in the thymus as an evolutionary accident of no very great significance." [3]

Not all scientists agreed on this notion; in fact, some believed otherwise. According to *Jacques F. A. P. Miller,* author of *"Revisiting Thymus Function"* [4] an article featured in the U.S. National Library of Medicine (NLM), the Center for Biotechnology Information (NCBI), and the National Institute of Health, prior to 1961, did not consider the thymus to have played any vital role in immunity.

It was not until later that research revealed that the prior arguments were fallible. Without the support of the thymus gland, the chances of children having a normal lifestyle are questionable. The thymus is at its largest in children and reduces in size with age. One of the primary functions of this organ is to produce autoimmune cells (T-cells) and supports the development of the immune system, which protects the body against harmful viral attacks.

Now since the organ is at its largest in children, what if it was considered vestigial and discarded during the early stages of child development? The adult body would not have a robust immune system and every other cell that depends on the thymus to secrete the right hormones at the right time would malfunction. This renders the body susceptible to becoming disease-prone and incapable of maintaining homeostasis.

I resolve that the argument for vestigial components is very limited, and at best, time should be the deciding factor. Yes, we know a lot, but we do not know it all. In the same breath, who knows when the "vestigial(s)" of the body of Christ will, under the right circumstances become the head cornerstone.

No one can tell you what you will become tomorrow. They may only speculate about today but tomorrow is a result that requires the process of today. Hint, hint, nudge, nudge, wink, wink…your purpose in life is to know yourself better than the world knows you, understand your function and get busy working at it. But before you can begin working at "it", you must have a correct perspective of self, your gifts, abilities and how to apply them. This becomes clearer for those who are connected to the Creator.

If you do not know who you are, the world will call you vestigial, when in fact you are a specialist! ***If you don't know who you are, any identification will do.*** Besides that of your Creator, the greatest knowledge you can ever obtain is of yourself. It reduces guessing and indecisiveness but drastically improves your precision and definiteness to pursue and achieve purpose.

> *"If you don't know which road to take, then any road will get you there."*
> ~Dr. Myles E. Munroe (1954-2014)

THE CASE AGAINST VESTIGIAL

"People who changed the world"

Usually, I am not a collector of anything, but one of my keepsakes is a magazine by *Newsweek*. The title "*100 People Who Shaped Our World*" [4] grabbed my attention and I could not resist when I saw it was the collectable special edition of their June-July 2015 issue. The cover was adorned with many prominent faces, including men and women of multicultural descendant and diverse backgrounds: scientists, inventors, machinist, politicians and public figures from television to Nobel Laureates and human rights activists. It reported on the one hundred people who help shaped our world. Among them was Jesus of Nazareth, who said, "*The greatest among you* (in the kingdom of God) *will be your servant* (are those who serve their gifts)." (Emphasis added, see Matthew 23:11).

This special edition consists of some of the world's greatest minds, many of whom society originally considered vestigial but became thought leaders who transformed the world. I have chosen to mention a few of them in this section. Each individual is classified vestigial on the basis of injustice he or she may have experienced: inequality due to gender or race, isolation as a result of societal labels, ill treatment and deprivation of resources or barred from opportunities that were otherwise normal for other humans. Many of these people and countless others are what society considers useless, unimportant and like a misunderstood organ of the body, should be discarded.

Among them is *Albert Einstein,* the distinguished Jewish physicist who had several learning disabilities including speech impairment. According to a documentary by the *History Channel*, Einstein's *"out of the box"* thought processes were discounted and rejected as being vestigial by the leaders of the science world of his time. He later became Professor Einstein and persevered to win the Nobel Prize in Physics. Today, his *"Theory of Relativity"* and $E=MC^2$ has become a household name in the world of science. It was Einstein who also said, *"I want to know the mind of God in the form of a mathematical equation."* [5] Many believed that the equation $E=MC^2$ was the supernatural response he received.

In another arena, anyone who's ever heard of a friendly mouse named Mickey also knew about the Magical World of Disney. Here we see another *"vestigial"* who was released from his job because they considered him *"mentally challenged, slow in creativity and imagination,"* the magazine reported. Today the name *Walt Disney* is synonymous with creativity and profound imagination.

Sidney Poitier became the first Black actor to receive an Oscar. Like all vestigial components where value is denounced before worth is uncovered, Poitier was told to *"Become a dishwasher"* instead of acting. Despite Hollywood's view of him, Poitier went from dishwashing to the center stage to the big screen and changed the world for many including people of color.

She was born a slave and in those times, slaves were the epitome of society's vestigials. *Harriet Tubman*, became the *"Moses of her people"* and the first *women conductor* of the road to freedom.

Jesus of Nazareth, his name remains a source of controversy among religious sects; some call him prophet, the *turn the other cheek fella* but his death on the cross made people, even his close followers believed that his work and ministry was completely over. But his resurrection launched a revolution that changed the course of history and impacts us even today. Now over three billion know him to be their teacher, healer, restorer, Lord and Savior.

Gender and equality were not always synonymous with society's view of women. *Susan B. Anthony* and *Elizabeth Cady Stanton* rewrote history and leveled the social and political playing fields between men and women alike. At a time when women were considered less than equal to men, both women were resilient in the struggle against inequality for women. Today they are forever remembered for their commitment to setting the record straight that *"We Are One."*

Nelson Mandela was society's vestigial abandonment for twenty-seven years, but became the first black president of a country once separated by hate and apartheid. Mandela not only transformed a nation on the premises of love and forgiveness, but he changed the mindset of the world against apartheid.

Oprah Winfrey was considered *"unfit for television news"* but later transformed the face of television to become one of the most influential black female billionaires in the world. Not only did Oprah change television, she *"OWN(s)"* it. Winfrey suffered as a child; consequently, her abusers did not consider her valuable, but she became a survivor and helped propose *"the Oprah Bill."* This bill was signed into law by former President

Bill Clinton as *The National Child Protection Act of 1993,* [6] a bill that created a nationwide database of child abusers.

Garrett Morgan, the self-educated son of a freed slave revolutionized the automobile industry and greatly defused the chaos of transportation with his invention of the *three-signal traffic light.* Morgan also invented the gas mask and other notable inventions.

Hundreds of other men and women changed the course of life forever. What would the world be like if they, like the vestigial components of the body, were discarded before their time? Thankfully, they persevered to become an indelible thread in the fabric of our world today. You are no different. Neither are you vestigial. You are a necessary part of life.

WHAT RESEARCH REVEALS

Apparently, I am not the only one who sees a major flaw in this *"Banged-up"* scientific theory of vestigial components. The Appendix was once believed to be vestigial, but researchers are now discovering that it houses bacterial cells that support the digestive system. In an online article published by the *National Geographic,* Jeffrey Laitman, director of anatomy and functional morphology at New York City's Mount Sinai School of Medicine and president-elect of the American Association of Anatomists considered the theory of having vestigial body parts a *"Dangerous Logic."*

I totally agree with his viewpoint because for years, scientists assured the public that removing an unwanted part from the body is visibly safe and that the body would still function with little deficiency. Clearly, this is neither wise nor functionally safe. According to Mr. Laitman, *"Whenever a body part is moved or changed, there's a price to pay."* [7]

My question is, are you ready to pay that price? And do you think the same thing happens to people who society considers to be *right-offs*, useless and as a result remove them from their community? This is the world we live in. However, there's great hope for the kingdom of God in the earth. Those people that were called vestigial could become world-changers, as was previously stated.

In another article by the *New York Times*, a team of Harvard Medical school researchers in conjunction with a group from *Massachusetts General Hospital* cited that the spleen has more value to the body than it is vestigial. One of the researchers, Dr. Matthias Nahrendorf said. *"The more you learn, the more you realize that we're just scratching on the surface of life. We don't know the whole story about anything."* [8] An organ that was once thought to be useless is now being hailed a lifeline and a legion of *"Monocyte"* soldiers who assist the body during severe traumatic events. The spleen, houses a multitude of immune cells, parked and simply waiting for the right time to be released into the bloodstream to defend the body. Dr. Nahrendorf calls these warrior cells *"A standing army,"* always on guard.

These vital immune cells do more than just protect the body against microbial attacks; they are builders and repair specialists of the body. *"They remove dead muscle cells, they start rebuilding stable scar tissue, they stimulate the generation of new blood vessels,"* said Dr. Nahrendorf. Monocytes are responsible for repairing the cardiac tissues after a heart attack (myocardial infarction) has occurred.

You see, unlike the world systems of religion where they discard and annul you because of your differences the body celebrates those differences and regards every human as a vital cell, tissue, or organ that plays an essential role in the circle of life and not a vestigial *"no-good."* In the anatomy of a kingdom community, *"different"* makes us special enough to be honored for the function we do in our area of giftedness.

Not all are equally gifted, but each part shares a vital function in keeping the body alive. Think of yourself as a member in the body, which has multiple interdependent systems that depend on each other to carry out their functions for the sole purpose of maintaining life. Specifically, body cells depend on the heart to pump blood, oxygen and nutrients in order for cells to work.

"Different" makes us special enough to be honored for the function we do in our area of expertise and giftedness."

The body structure depends on the skeletal systems for support; likewise, the nervous system allows the body to sense and respond to its environment, while the muscular system connects to the bones and skeletal system to provide movement. Is the picture of the kingdom becoming a lot clearer to you now?

"Christ is also the head of the church, which is his body." (Colossians 1:18 NLT) You too are part of a supernatural design created to function with a specific purpose as you use your gift in a community-body of Christ called the *"church"* to reflect the glory of God in the earthly realm. *"Each of you*

should use whatever gift you have received to serve others, as faithful stewards of God's grace in its various forms" (1 Peter 4:10). Likewise, each body cell serves a specific function, while body systems represent groups of people in specific communities who use their gifts to serve others. This design is visible throughout every creation on earth, so long as it is alive, and has cells, tissues, organs, organ systems and an organism called a body.

You don't have to look very far to understand that this concept of the kingdom of God in motion is all around you.

It is not the amount you have, but your willingness to use what you have been given that matters

---

Just look in the mirror, touch yourself, move, think, breath and you will discover that you are an amazing creation who came from a supernatural creator. Now let's take a closer look at your anatomy to help you make this very important connection between the body's anatomy and physiology and the kingdom of God as systems of function.

GLIMPSE OF YOUR COMPLEXITY

The complexity of your internal design is a wonder to behold. The human body is one unit with many members that carry out many different functions based on their giftedness. It is one of the most complex creation on earth. Although God in all his Omniscience is the ultimate creator, through creation, he has made a way for humankind to have a glimpse of his mind. The field of science has revolutionized the world through *S.T.E.M* (*Science, Technology, Engineering, and Math*) and its systemic approach to solving world issues.

Likewise, the body has a built-in method that allows it to adjust to changes and correct its internal environment. This process has a specific method of operating within guidelines that were designed and set forth by God for the sole purpose of extending his kingdom to earth.

Remember, everything belongs to God…*"For the earth is the Lord's and everything in it"* (1 Corinthians 10:26). This includes the knowledge I'm sharing with you right now. He gets all the glory, praise and honor. In return, I experience the JOY of being a willing and active participant in this whole process. I'm no expert, I assure you. I am just like you, a member in the body who decided to function and in doing so you benefit. This is the will of God for every human. Just use what you have. The Kingdom is not based on quantity but quality. It is not the amount you have, but your willingness to use what you have been given.

Most of us doubt that we could make any difference in the world. Don't look at the world, start with yourself and then your community, your city and country. Just start somewhere. You don't need another degree or PhD to impact and transform lives…just desire. Find your gift and begin to function and watch your life change instantly, right before your eyes.

Regardless of how insignificant the gift may look, everyone has something to offer that could dramatically change the world for good. Remember when the disciples became anxious because they did not know how or where they would get enough food to feed the people? A little boy donated his *five loaves and two fish* to feed a multitude of people. (See Matthew 14:21). Who knows what great adventures God has in store for you? There's only one way to find out.

Start today. Take an inventory of your life, awaken your dormant gifts and put them into action to serve others as a function. The result could surprise you because the kingdom of God is all about function. Each active participant is designed to serve the other. To preserve, maintain and prosper the citizens who live and abide by the laws that govern God's kingdom.

NOTES

Chapter 3: Kingdom Culture and the Body Systems

1. MacLean LD, Zak SJ, Varco RL, Good RA. The role of the thymus in Antibody production: an experimental study of the immune response in thymectomized rabbits. Transplant Bull (1956) 4:21–2 [PubMed] 5 Apr. 2015
2. Miller, Jacques F. A. P. "Revisiting Thymus Function." *Frontiers in Immunology*514):411. *PMC*.Web. http://www.ncbi.nlm.nih.gov/pmc/articles/PMC4147245/ 5 Apr. 2015.
3. Medawar PB. Discussion after Miller JFAP and Osoba D. Role of the thymus in the origin of immunological competence. In: Wolstenholme GEW, Knight J, editors. The Immunologically Competent Cell: Its Nature and Origin. (Vol. 16), London: Ciba Foundation Study Group; (1963). 70 p.
4. Labs, Media. "100 People Who Shaped Our World." *Newsweek Magazine Special Ed.* July 2015. Print.
5. *Einstein.* (DOCUMENTRY) Perf. Albert Einstein. *History Channel, History.com.* Https://www.youtube.com/watch?v=N0x9gApvuGo. Web. 01 Aug. 15.
6. Assoc. Press. "THE NATIONAL CHILD PROTECTION ACT 1993." *The New York Times National.* New York Times, Vachss.com, 21 Dec. 1993. Web. http://www.vachss.com/mission/president.html. 07 July 2013.
7. Koerth-Baker, Maggie. "Vestigial Organs Not So Useless After All, Studies Find." *National Geographic.* National Geographic Society, 30 July 2009. Web. 01 Sept. 2013.
8. ANGIER, NATALIE. "Finally, the Spleen Gets Some Respect." *Nytimes.com/SCIENCE.* New York Times, 3 Aug. 2009. Web. http://www.nytimes.com/2009/08/04/science/04angier.html. 15 Aug. 2015.
9. Clayton, Julie. "Lymphocytes: Not Useless after All." *The Journal of Experimental Medicine.* The Rockefeller University Press, 20 Mar. 2006. Web. 22 Sept. 2013.

CHAPTER 4

KNOWING YOUR GIFT MAKES WAY
Your gift makes you Unique, Irresistible and Irreplaceable
~ Andrew E. Guy

Everyone has a gift, a function and a purpose. Just by taking a moment from your busy day to sit down and analyze your anatomy, you will be amazed at how complex and well organized your physiology is. Your body is an organism, made of organ systems, which are made of organs, which are made of tissues, which comes from cells made of atoms created by God. The beauty of all this is that they are all interconnected and you get to play a vital part in all of this.

Hang in there, there's more.

Your Freedom to Function comes from knowing your gift

The *real church* is no different. Like these organs, which are diversely made of many to become one, so is the body of Christ, a diversely complex group of specialized people who are gifted to serve each other in the body called a community. The power of choice makes you a free agent, but your abilities and *your freedom to function comes from knowing your gift.* Financial freedom does not make you FREE, however, it gives you more options to use your gift to transform the world and have a greater impact on humanity.

Money makes things easier and provides you with access to more resources, but it is your gift when used for the glory of God, that makes you prosperous and brings ultimate freedom. *"Seek the Kingdom of God above all else, and live righteously, and he will give you everything you need"* (Matthew 6:33 NLT). It is in the Kingdom where you find your gift and once discovered everything you need comes as a result. All things necessary are added to you in order to support the full functioning of the gift. Your gift is what makes you *unique, irresistible and irreplaceable.* It is neither your religion nor how well you pray, it is the gift of God, which paves the way and makes your Creator a visible presence in this world.

PRINCIPLE OF USING YOUR GIFT

So who are you in the body? Have you thought about this yet? I trust that by the end of this book, you will discover the answers to your life that will make living crystal clear. One of my primary goals for this project is to be as explicitly detailed as possible in our explanation about the role of science and the intricate design of the human body. How its interconnected functions mirror the kingdom of God as a community-body called his *church*.

Furthermore, it is my hope that you begin to see church not as a religious practice where you attend periodically, but as a living community of people (the image of God) where you serve your gift as a special function in a dark world. God is glorified through your service as you *let your light shine!*

Principles you must understand and commit to memory:

(1) Church is not a place.
(2) People in a shared community is the church personified.
(3) The practice of religion does not glorify God.
(4) Interconnectedness is the foundation of the kingdom.
(5) Function is the way to fulfill God's purpose in the earth.
(6) Everyone wins when we function.
(7) Life is a gift but living is a process of many functions.
(8) God is the producer and revealer of ALL knowledge.
(9) Faith is a precursor to belief that requires action.
(10) Words are the substance of everything created.

Your life is no accident and your living should not be one either

Everything in the kingdom is interconnected and each connection, big or small, serves a vital purpose in the completion and overall functioning of the kingdom. This supernatural orchestration is designed to manifest the ultimate purpose of the king: to create a kingdom in the earthly realm just like the one in Jehovah's heavenly realm. I call this the *ultimate design.* A design so perfect that it has become the blueprint for everything created on earth.

The anatomical structure and function of the human body is a direct replica and by far, the greatest analogy of the kingdom on earth. Despite their levels of visibility, everything in the human body is interconnected and is vital to the livelihood of every human being. Even after you die, your remains still serve a purpose in providing nutrients to the plants that provides more oxygen to sustain life on earth. Only God could orchestrate such an amazing blueprint.

The body is the kingdom of God in motion and you are all a part of it. Be they macro or microscopic, known or unknown, discovered or undiscovered, every cell is vital to the overall functioning of the body. They all work together to maintain a common balance that scientist(s) call homeostasis. As a result, no part of the body should be considered vestigial (useless or none-function-specific) or insignificant. Every joint supplies the other, every tissue supports the other and every nerve innervates a structure that carries out a function for one purpose only—to maintain homeostasis or oneness throughout the body.

Your life is no accident and your living should not be one either. Remember, God is not the author of disorder or confusion. And wherever there is homeostasis, there is both balance and order. He is right there in the midst. Where two or three, even four or more are assembled, God is present and it is he who makes the connection between the parts possible.

We are all instruments of the divine king with special gifts, unlimited abilities and untapped potentials. Our function-specific skills are necessary to maintaining the quality of life that displays the glory of the one *real* God, the ultimate creator and king. Anyone who tells you differently has no earthly idea who they are (a kingdom in motion), where they came from (the mind of God) or where they're going (to replicate the function and purpose of the kingdom of God on earth). In other words, the world should know God when they interact with you. Period.

GIFTS TO SERVE

You were created to serve. It is through this function that your meaning for living is discovered. Some of the greatest people to ever walk the planet are those who didn't just serve, they became servants to their gift. The world is shaped and transformed by people who used their gifts.

No religion can teach you how to serve. It is already inside of you and part of your makeup. You are made for service. Your creator promised to give you the desires of your heart and that promise has already been granted. The function of *service* is part of your makeup; it is in you, and it is one of your *"priorities."*

Steven R. Covey wrote a book called *"First Things First,"* [1] a very powerful book about how to attain success by prioritizing your life; however, I believe our *"First Things First"* should be to seek first the kingdom (God's direction) and the discovery of our purpose, then a will to connect and serve our gifts. If you want to be great, choose to serve.

If you refuse to serve you refuse to function. And if you fail to function the body will die. And if you die, you would have missed an amazing opportunity to change the world.

Collectively, everything is embedded inside of us but no one person, cell, tissue or system has everything it needs to survive; nor does it exist by itself or for itself.

When you function, you establish, promote and maintain life in an earthly community called the body. This is why all living things, humans especially, have the same internal order of functions; "*ACTOOO*" (atoms, cells, tissues, organs, organ systems, and organism), the anatomy and physiology that makes up the organism.

Bruce Lee, who brought the gift of martial arts to the masses once said, *"The only way humans become different and have a "new style", is if they have three legs and three arms."* [2] I could not agree more.

PURPOSE-BASED DIFFERENTIATION

Religion teaches us to seek out the differences in humanity and penalize people for it. But when was the last time you looked at another human and saw him walking on his head (*cephalic*), had legs for arms, their calves (*gastrocnemius*) were in the position of the shin bones (*tibia*) and had a knee cap (*patella*) for a heart? When was the last (or first) time you saw a human with wings or a fish with legs?

The answer is, never. If you need help differentiating another human being from an animal, simply look in the mirror, give yourself a huge hug and then give the *real* God praise. I still find it a miracle that God can create two different creatures with such close proximities and yet are one *hundred percent* different in nature. Humans are neither a higher form of monkeys nor their next of kin. As close as the chimpanzee is to having some traits of human characteristics, there's no comparison. Though feature may have some linking, a human is a human and an animal is simply, an animal.

Still scientists conclude that both animals and humans are relatives. To some extent we may have similar internal structures like eyes, heart, lung, and kidneys that enable the animal to carry out identical body functions as humans do. Both humans and animals breathe oxygen and come from the same Creator, God, the source of all life. But humans are vastly different from animals in terms of their behavioral, mental and spiritual capacity.

A MEANING "FULL" LIFE

It is my hope that by the time you are finished reading this book you will become fully aware of the function of God's kingdom operating in your body and life. *Every breath you take, every step you take and every decision you make is because of a kingdom authenticated, supernatural design.* We live in a world where institutions and the institutionalization of human behavior have become the *norm* of coping with the nuances of everyday living. And while life remains a gift, it is the process of living that brings about the many challenges we face as we attempt to deal with reality and make sense of it all.

"Live with meaning, anything less is simply trial and error and a costly experiment called effort"

God's Kingdom is at work within you, right now. The bible frequently uses the body as a representation of the kingdom of God. Ephesians chapter four talks about having unity in the body and how each of us is diversely gifted in order to create unity in the body as we serve each other. In other words, the body of Christ is the physical Kingdom of God on earth. Each person represents a bodily function as each joint lends its support to build up the body in unity for the sole purpose of manifesting the mind of God in the earth.

"From whom the whole body fitly joined together and compacted by that which every joint supplieth, according to the effectual working in the measure of every part, maketh increase of the body unto the edifying of itself in love." (Ephesians 4:16)
Your life will change drastically and be more meaningful once you become aware of this concept of the kingdom in motion—the living, breathing, you.

Living was not designed to be a mystery, difficult, or without meaning. Your life is a gift and your living was supernaturally designed to be a process that brings honor and glorifies the Creator of the life you live. Anything less is simply a trial and error and a costly experiment called effort. *You are a supernatural creation with a specific intention to operate spiritually and to physically manifest (make known or visible) the mind of the Creator.*

In the world of *S.T.E.M* (Science, Technology, Engineering, and Math), the term specification is used to describe a blueprint. A blueprint is the governing guide or system that determines the purpose and predicts the design and specific functioning of a product. With a supernaturally perfected blueprint (God-breathed), one can replicate the original product of the creator through purpose and function.

Likewise, the purpose of this book is to help you understand the Kingdom of God as a replicated (copy) of the human body as it relates to a supernatural design, its physical attributes, including its function and purpose as we relate to others in our selected area of influence or region known as a community.

I'm convinced that the world would be a better place if you knew who you were and how your gifts and abilities strategically fit into making others better. Remember, life is a gift, and *living should not be trial and error and a costly experiment called effort, but one of function and purpose that makes living "full" of meaning.*

"PRINCIPLES OF A GIFT"

- If you knew yourself, you'd know your Creator, and your function and purpose for living is not too far off.

- If you know the spirit, the fruit is not too far

- If you know the machine, the manufacturer is not too far.

- If you know the player, the coach is not too far.

- If you know the student, the teacher is not too far.

- If you know the child, the parent is not too far.

- If you know the behavior, character is not too far.

- If you *"overstood"* your gifts, the weight of understanding how to use them would become lighter, and living with meaning is not too far.

- If you knew how close you were to destiny, quitting would be the farthest thing from your mind.

NOTES

Chapter 10. Kingdom Culture and the Body Systems

1. Covey, Stephen R., A. Roger. Merrill, and Rebecca R. Merrill. *First Things First: To Live, to Love, to Learn, to Leave a Legacy*. New York: Simon & Schuster, 1994. Print.

2. *The Mandarin Superstar*. Perf. Bruce Lee, Pierre Berton. *Documentary/interview*. The Pierre Berton Show, 12 Sept. 1971. Web. 16 Apr. 2016.

PART- II

THE POWER OF COMMUNITY: THE KINGDOM IN MOTION
"Interconnected Success"

Life is a gift and living is choice-driven but learning is a shared process.
~Andrew E. Guy

CHAPTER 5

POWER OF COMMUNITY

Beyond religion, community is one of the greatest assembled forces on planet earth. As a result, the wealth and power of any community is not found in the infrastructure, architectural appearances, technological advances or monetary resources, but in the people. Think of it this way: *a product is only as valuable as the parts from which it is made.* Therefore, the building blocks that create the foundation of all communities are its people.

Without people, there is no community; without community, there is no assembled force and without God, there is no power source. People make the world go 'round; not resources by themselves, people do. In fact, the greatest resource on planet earth is people. I believe the following extract best illustrates this point:

> *"If you leave a one hundred dollar bill in the middle of Time Square, New York, all things held constant, (and there are no sticky fingers within a one million mile radius of that bill), it will remain there unused, untouched, undeveloped and without growth.*

> *'Unless a human with a success mindset puts this one hundred dollar bill into productive action, nothing will happen. Bottom line, it is vital that you see people as an essential part."* (Guy, Andrew E., Work Your Words: Finding your pathway to personal success, Gladshare Media Publishing, 2015)

So when are humans most powerful? Simple, when they are serving. Jesus summed it up best when he said, *"The greatest in the kingdom of God are those who serve"* (Matthew 23:11).

God has given each of us the ability to display his power in the earth, but the choice is ours to activate and utilize these abilities. Your gift is like a powerful light source to light the world, but it requires a switch to activate its resources to shine. The Holy Spirit is the switch but it is the function of the kingdom in you that produces the light.

If your gift is not activated you will remain dormant and ineffective, having a form of giftedness without the power. Here's another way to look at this principle. Your body is a small community of many systems derived from atoms, cells, tissues and organs that jointly function as one cohesive unit.

If a finite value were to be assigned to the human body and it's building blocks, which would you consider to be the most valuable? The body or its components? The components would have the greater value because without the building blocks there would be no body. In essence, people are the vital components that add value to a community-body. In the same manner, the components that make up the human body are servants to a larger system.

Through service we have "*shared*" dominion; not to control each other, but rather, to "have" control over things, circumstances and events.

A HEART TO SERVE

We are all "*...fearfully and wonderfully made: marvelous are thy works; and that my soul knoweth right well*" according to Psalm 139:14 (KJV). And here's the best part, no one has to convince YOU about your identity; deep down, our souls know this. There's a spiritual part of us that identifies with our unique abilities and specialized gifts, but knowing is not enough; there must be more than just thought—a heart of serving must become a real and tangible part of your lifestyle. Service is at the core of every community. This is what we were created to do—*establish the kingdom of God on earth through our service to others*. The world has no idea what this is; much less, how to do this and what it should look like when it is done from a place of purity without extrinsic rewards.

THE GOAL OF COMMUNITY

Think about this. Have you ever wondered what the number one goal of every person on earth is? I'll tell you. It is not about the haves and have not's, rich or poor and classism. Absolutely not; it is to be in a shared community (gated or not, city or suburb, country or trailer park, bush or beach, penthouse or basement, hood or ghetto) where they can share resources and serve their gifts and expertise. Although it meets a deep need to feel safe, cared for, loved and respected, community also offers a unified partnership of likeminded people who are purpose driven. Most people think that the goal of getting rich is to be well-known and famous; no, it is to create a life that empowers people to freely serve their gifts and expertise to others.

The shared commonwealth of the kingdom allows every citizen to have access to the abundant resources in their community. *"At the present time your plenty will supply what they need, so that in turn their plenty will supply what you need. The goal is equality"* (2 Corinthians 8:14).

LIVE TO SERVE

No one person is self-sufficient; everyone has something the next person needs. Community sustains us and we are indeed, our brother's keeper. It is my desire that you be at your best whenever you serve. This is the core longing of every human being on earth. It is not only the ultimate desire, it is our calling.

Through service, we are fulfilled and renewed daily. As a result, the servant is rewarded for faithfully serving his gift. Remember, success in life is not about your looks or the amount of degrees on your wall or letters after your name; rather, it is *really* about how diligent you are at using the matter that resides between your two ears, your brain.

Humans are created to give and they are wired to serve. One of our greatest fulfillments is experienced when we serve. Do you remember how you felt the last time you did something out of a purely unselfish place in your heart for someone? The sense of gratitude that flooded your heart and made you want to do it again, and again, and again…? The reason why you feel such a positive rush and a great sense of accomplishment when you do something that transforms someone's life, is because service is directly connected to your purpose for living.

THE EFFECTS OF MALFUNCTION

You function correctly when you serve, but you malfunction when you are unable to contribute to the growth and well-being of others. The effects of malfunction is grossly felt when you cannot serve others; your inability creates a void and a feeling of uselessness in your spirit that leads to frustration, fatigue and even depression. A sensation of helplessness overwhelms you. Just imagine the wounded soldier who is unable to fight for his country or a parent who is incapable of providing for their children—devastating.

But imagine this also, having the power, the capacity and the ability to serve but you choose not to. Withholding a necessity that brings life and support to others is *"Community-Suicide."* What would happen if your heart decides not to beat or pump blood to other body cells? Death is inevitable. Community therefore, becomes a living organism where everyone plays a vital role to sustain the whole. Without community, gifts remain dormant, purpose unmet, destiny forfeited and God becomes invisible. This is not God's plan.

THE ORIGINAL PLAN

God's original purpose was for ALL mankind to use their gifts to serve in his kingdom. Service, in the kingdom sense, means using your gift or area of expertise to provide a service that completes a process and makes the body of your community whole. The fall of Adam and Eve changed that but God did not change his plan. He placed his gift in every human with a purpose to contribute to the optimal functioning of the earth that was under the ruler-ship of mankind. Originally, God created humans with a pure heart. The use and perfecting of each gift was intended to produce homeostasis—God's kingdom in motion in the earth.

However, the latter is not taking place among humanity even though the gifts are still inside each of us: *"But we have this treasure in <u>earthen vessels</u> that the excellency of the power may be of God, and not of us"* 2 Corinthians 4:7 (KJV). The same verse is worded slightly different in another translation: *"But we have this treasure in <u>jars of clay</u> to show that this all-surpassing power is from God and not from us."* 2 (Corinthians 4:7 NIV).

Everyone has this gift (heavenly treasure inside) to serve humanity, even those who have not made Jesus Christ their Lord and King. Individually, we may be *jars of clay*, but together and as a community, we are fields with buried *treasures* waiting to be discovered and used.

I can only imagine how sublime and awe-inspiring living would be if we let our lights shine to glorify Jehovah God by serving others. There are benefits to using your gift when you have Jesus as your Lord versus being gifted and void of purpose. God empowers us and orders our steps for guaranteed success. Without him, we are like wandering gifts and dim light bulbs having unlimited brightness but remain in darkness, incapable of lighting a pathway for the world to see. Full of use, but completely *used-less*.

There's more to serving than just having a gift. You need knowledge, wisdom and direction, and these come as benefits of being connected to your Creator. After all, he is the creator of the product *(you)* and he knows how to make *you* work optimally and for his glory. Being gifted and without God is similar to having a brand new turbo racing car, but with the wrong set of keys you will not be able to activate the engine to extract the ***power-of-drive*** that is trapped within its pistons. You will remain parked.

When you use your gift without God, the gift, which was supposed to be a blessing becomes a toilsome burden and a destructive force that destroys you and others. While some have unfortunately, resorted to very selfish and destructive use of their gifts, there are still some practical ways that we can and do serve others in a community that have enhanced the way we live. There are multiple ways that community benefits all of us, but the most powerful aspects of serving others is built on relationships. Serving benefits everyone in a community and here are some examples:

SUCCESS IN BUSINESS

The power of community can be applied to the world of business, where each person is a stakeholder of the organization/company. Here, serving is a major key to enhancing the community. Imagine the kingdom of God as a multi-trillion dollar company where the total value of the company is based on the giftedness of each stakeholder involved with the company. Next, envision that the infinite profitability of the company is determined by the faithfulness and usefulness of each stakeholder's ability to unselfishly serve their talents for the betterment of the organization.

Now let's assume you were the CEO of this multi-trillion dollar company and your job-function is critical to the maintenance and advancement of your company—if everything comes to a screeching halt when you are on vacation, what do you think will happen when you retire? The company will fail miserably. This is why serving our gifts, talents, skills and abilities are a vital part of creating a lasting community in any company or organization.

Because everyone plays an essential role in the overall success of the company, the ship should not capsize in the absence of the CEO. Ideally, this is how it should be, but the reality is not always ideal. Oftentimes, companies still fail whether the CEO is present or absent, but this is mainly due to lack of effective leadership. On the other hand, effective leaders are present even in their absence: their exemplary lifestyles, principles and sound judgements remain long after they are gone. The next chapter provides the details on this type of leadership from Moses' perspective.

LEAD-IT-FORWARD

So how can we apply the concept of the community to reduce the frequency of failure in businesses today and in the future? Through the process of *self-replication*. By keeping the next generation in mind, systems of operation should undergo continuous improvement to ensure greater success for its future. A great way for companies to do this is to *lead-it-forward*: to always train qualified successors and exemplary protégés to carry on the legacy of those before them. The willingness to serve and grow is the key to future success.

Therefore, the foundation of all successful companies is built on having a *service-centered* team that is able to replicate its strengths in the next generation. And the more equipped the individual components are, the stronger the organization will be.

SUCCESS IN THE CHURCH

First, it is important that you understand that the *"real"* church is not a building where people assemble on weekends to listen to a preacher, give money, shake hands, get rid of yesterday's guilt and sing songs when it is convenient to attend. No; this may be the perception of modern-day religion, but the church which is the body of Christ operating in the earth to reveal God's glory, is a community and a living organism made up of a diverse group of people with specific gifts. **The real church is alive: it breathes, it feels and responds to stimuli.**

Second, as we have previously discussed in **Part One,** the body of Christ is similar to the human body. It has vital signs and various structures (cells and organs) that carry out specific functions to maintain life, just like the church. The *"community-church"* has similar structures in the form of people, with functions in the form of specific gifts to establish, strengthen and maintain every area of this community-body of Christ known as the church. With these elements present, success in the church is very possible. But let's examine the process of how to really make this happen.

Life is a gift and living is choice-driven but learning is a shared process.

~Andrew E. Guy

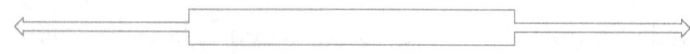

CHAPTER 6

TOGETHER WE WIN

*If we are not winning the fight of relationship,
We are losing the battle of community.*
~Andrew E. Guy

This same biological concept applies to the church. As a body it has a person (structure) or groups of people (organs) who are the heart, some legs, others brain, ears and eyes for the edification of the church. They are physical duties but are spiritually discerned and are known as *Ministries*. In essence, they do exactly what the word says; they "minister" or serve the church body and provide everything it needs so there would be no lack.

In theory, the church has everything it needs, but in a practical sense, it is grossly deficient in multiple ways. This is evident because there is a persistent lack of knowledge. If several members have a gift and the church has no idea, nor can these people be identified by their functions, then it would appear as if the gifts were absent from the body and (*MIF*) *missing in function* and void of God's glory.

The church is one BIG puzzle with all the pieces present, but we must put the puzzle together to make the whole body of Christ a completely functional unit. *"There are different kinds of gifts, but the same Spirit...different kinds of service, (ministries) but the same Lord...different kinds of working, but the same God works in all of them in all men"* (1 Corinthians 12:4-6).

Everyone has a piece of the puzzle and the gifts to supply every need for the common good, but this is not possible if people are not coming together. Division and obstruction of divine purpose are the works of the enemy. If he can just keep you separated, (divide and conquer) he wins while you struggle.

Through the spirit of division, many have gone their own separate ways in search of a God who has never left. Religion (which is discussed in the next section), is all man-made. Ironically, this channel which was created to direct us to oneness with God, has become so infinitely sub-divided that there hardly appears to be any visible trace of God left in the earth.

When the world sees this, they say in their hearts, *"I see no God. Where is he? Where is the power and the glory you preach of? I drive a Benz and live in a mansion on the hill. What do you have? Show me your God and the works of your faith."* The truth is that wealth, material goods and inherited status is neither an accurate reflection nor representation of Godliness or righteousness if the body is divided within itself. A body divided is a *"no-body"* and a lifeless corpse; and **God divided is god-less-ness, but God together is ONE in body and mind, in spirit and truth.**

ENVISION THE UNITY

Just imagine what would happen if we were one united body: *what a community, what a city, what a country, what a nation, what a world and what a people we would be!* We must come together to have the victory in our communities. All it takes is two: where two or three are gathered, God is infinitely multiplied (not divided) and if we simply touch and agree on...ANYTHING (Are you ready for this?) it is done! Togetherness is the thread that makes up the fabric of every society and it is an essential part of all communities.

The world does not need more church *buildings*; what they desperately seek are examples, followed by signs, miracles, wonders and the demonstrated power of God through the lives of the believers. Jesus said signs would follow those who believe. For example, "*...They will place their hands on sick people and they will get well*" (Mark 16:18*b*). The signs he's speaking of are tangible examples of the abundant life overflowing in the life of the believer. Without any proof of power, the church appears dominated instead of having dominion and the name of God becomes a public disgrace. The church struggles to have any influence. It spends countless hours fasting and praying to God for a personal miracle instead of creating lasting change to positively transform themselves and their communities.

Paul provides a clear and precise description on the type of oneness God requires of us in a kingdom-community: "*And he gave some, apostles; and some, prophets; and some, evangelists; and some, pastors and teachers; For the perfecting of the saints...Till we all come in the unity of the faith...unto a perfect man..."* Ephesians 4:11-13 *(KJV)*.

The kingdom-community on earth is designed to be equipped with everything it needs to grow and thrive even in the presence of the enemy. With Christ as our head, Paul also wrote that: *"...the whole body fitly joined together and compacted by that which every joint supplieth, according to the effectual working...of every part, maketh increase of the body unto the edifying of itself in love."* Ephesians 4:16 *(KJV)*

AWARENESS IS VITAL

A body that is unaware that it has eyes will never see, and never walk if it has no idea it has legs, and never think if it does not know it possesses brainpower. This is the modern-day church. But there is still hope and a remedy for victory in the kingdom community-church. It begins with leaders who have a keen awareness to discern the spiritual eyes, ears, hearts and minds in their churches—find them, know their function, activate their gifts and put them to work for the benefit of the body. It is vital that you get this, especially if you are a pastor or leader in your organization.

WISE COUNSEL ON LEADERSHIP

One of the greatest leaders of the bible who exudes this quality of superb leadership was Nehemiah, the king's cupbearer who became the governor of Jerusalem and rebuilt the city walls. He had a great love for his community, visual acuity, understanding of people's skill-set and keen ability to assemble a team of people and use them to complete a task that brought glory to God. (I suggest you read the entire book of Nehemiah).

Leadership is crucial in the body of Christ because the church is a living organism that needs the supportive nutrients of everyone to provide order and maintain homeostasis. God's church is designed similar to the section in the previous chapter on *Success in Business,* where the kingdom is a *"multi-trillion"* dollar company, having a CEO and stakeholders. Most churches operate under the *"Top-down"* methodology, where the pastor is the head and everyone else is under him or her. This approach is the least effective because it leads to "pastoral-burnout", stress related illnesses and a malnourished church body.

Leadership is crucial but wise counsel saves lives. Every leader must lead with the understanding that not everyone you lead will believe in your leadership or your vision for change. In fact, some of your greatest struggles will come from those who attempt to follow you.

Moses of the bible learned this all too well. After leading the Israelites out of Egypt, he became extremely exhausted and struggled to maintain order in the camp of his congregation as the people quarreled and contended with him. In the second verse of Exodus 17, Moses responded: *"Why do you quarrel with me? Why do you test the LORD?"* Moses was their leader and everyone turned to him for help with their personal, family or communal disputes. As the pressure mounted, *Moses cried out to the LORD, "What am I to do with these people? They are almost ready to stone me."* (Exodus 17:4) It was not until Jethro, Moses' father-in-law, the Midianite Priest, visited him in the desert and counselled him in the way of horizontal leadership that Moses' life and leadership skills were dramatically transformed.

We pick up the story of Moses and the Israelites in Exodus 18:13-14: as Moses sat to judge the people from morning to evening, Jethro became very concerned and confronted him saying, *"What is this you are doing for the people and why do you do it alone?"* Moses tried explaining to his father-in-law the reason for doing what he thought was a good thing, but the Midianite Priest would hear none of it. Verse 17-18 reads: *"What you are doing is not good…you and these people who come to you will only wear yourselves out. The work is too heavy for you; you cannot handle it alone,"* said Jethro.

After rebuking his son-in-law, Jethro instructed Moses about his divine responsibility and the power of delegation through horizontal leadership. *"Let me give you some advice, and may God be with you,"* he said. *"If you do this and God so commands, you will be able to stand the strain, and all these people will go home satisfied"* (Exodus 18:19a). Remember, **leadership is crucial but wise counsel saves lives, including yours.**

Effective leadership requires more than just one's ability to lead others; it is also incumbent upon that leader to seek wise counsel and credible information that equips and empowers the leader to lead with diligence and understanding. Jethro's invaluable advice was instrumental to Moses because he could now approach leadership in a more effective way. Jethro instructed his "son" to do the following:

> *"You must be the people's representative before God and bring their disputes to him. Teach them his decrees and*

instructions, and show them the way they are to live and how they are to behave. ***But select capable men from all the people****—men who fear God, trustworthy men who hate dishonest gain—and appoint them as officials over thousands, hundreds, fifties and tens.* ***Have them serve*** *as judges for the people at all times, but have them bring every difficult case to you; the simple cases they can decide themselves. That will* ***make your load lighter, because they will share it with you"*** (Exodus 18:19b-22).

Following Jethro's advice, *"Moses listened to his father-in-law and did everything he said"* (Exodus 18:24). The work that God has for each of us is a monumental task and he did not intend for us to do it by ourselves.

Remember, a tabletop is held up by the amount of supporting legs beneath the table (people) who share the load of the top horizontally. The effectiveness of horizontal leadership makes it possible for every leader to empower others to have shared responsibility in their community. When you lead horizontally with others in mind, your difficult undertakings become simplified. It is also imperative that leaders know their assignment (what you are called to do) versus the role they play.

You were not called to do everything. The assignment is the purpose for your leadership and your role in this position is to educate those you lead; teaching them principles that **m**otivate, **i**nspire, **t**ransform and **e**ducate. Therefore, teaching is by far one of the most important roles of any leader. You must be able to skillfully communicate credible information to those you lead.

Noticed one of Jethro's primary instructions to Moses was to **teach the people.** See verse (20) *"Teach them his decrees and instructions, and show them the way they are to live and how they are to behave."* A community is informed through teaching, but the mindsets and behaviors of people are transformed by *wise counsel and modeled leadership.* In other words, your teaching must be a practical part of your life, so that those you lead can mirror what you live.

Even though Moses was doing what he thought was a good thing, it was killing him. Always remember this, ***a good thing is not always the right thing, even though it can always be improved upon and made better and even the best; but right is absolute and is transferable to every generation.***

Leadership requires balance in the form of spiritual, mental, and physical fitness. The lack of balance is detrimental to any church body or organization because *a weary and exhausted leader makes a terrible interpreter of divine instructions.* In the end, everyone suffers. The true purpose of leadership is to allow those who follow you to experience the kingdom of God through you. After all, it is God who appointed you and he alone should get the glory. You on the other hand receive the joy and the pleasure of serving.

There should be no grandstanding or self-glorification. On another occasion, Moses failed to give God the glory and willfully disobeyed him by striking the rock instead of speaking God's instructions (see Numbers 20:8). God will always put leaders in position (roles) so he (God) can be glorified, not you.

Effective leadership is a *community-shared* responsibility and not a one-man show. Many churches fail because their leaders see themselves as a cornerstone and the go-to person for the church body, so they become the burden bearer for everything that the church needs and experiences. *Remember, leaders must know who the spiritual eyes, ears, hearts and minds are in their churches; find them, know their function, activate their gifts and put them to work for the benefit of the body.* Shared responsibility and serving is paramount to everyone's success. One pastor is not able to meet the needs of every member; this leads to failure, chaos and community alienation.

On the contrary, the church stands a better chance at having a greater influence on people in the communities they chose to serve if it is committed to people-first instead of a religion. But in order to be successful, there are some *"first-things"* that must be established.

CULTIVATE COMMUNITY FIRST

All churches have the power to be successful at serving people and every leader has the necessary support inside the body to maintain order and lead more people to the kingdom. Cultivating a community does not mean converting people to a religion, but to introduce them to God's kingdom where they can build lasting relationships with people who are ready to use their gifts to serve others for the good of the entire community and for the glory of God.

The first step to establishing and maintaining a church body is to *cultivate a culture of community for every member.* Simply start by just loving people because they are people; not based on their status, influence or affluence, just love them.

This is how the world will know that you have the Spirit of God: *"By this all men will know that you are my disciples* (examples in the earth) *if you love one another"* (John 13:35). Real community is built on relationships not a religion or denomination. Also remember that while everyone has a gift and is fully equipped and furnished by God to serve each other, we are all encouraged to desire LOVE, the greatest gift. (See 1 Corinthians 12:31).

Why? Because love covers a multitude of faults and shatters the lenses of the *"judgmental-microscopes"* we use to focus on the problems and not the promises. Instead we see only the evil and not the good in others.

Secondly, instead of the *"Top-Down"* methodology, leaders must adopt the *"Horizontal"* approach to leading and mentoring their congregation or groups. The horizontal approach has a *"WE"* identity: it says, *"WE"* are the church; *"WE"* are in this together; *"WE"* are a community-family and *"WE"* all need each other to serve at our optimum best. **You sharpen me. I sharpen you. And together we change the world.** When churches cultivate winning communities, everybody wins! God gets the glory and each individual experiences the joy of serving and using his or her gifts for a much greater good: *people*.

Thirdly, it takes every member to make the church a living organism because the horizontal approach is *service-based*. It says, *"Everyone"* is necessary and the more of us there are serving the better it will be. This approach sees every member as a leg beneath the table that supports the (tabletop) kingdom, the mission, vision and purpose of the church as a whole.

Even better, horizontal leadership sees each community member as a stakeholder with a specific gift that meets a need in the whole body. In this, your light will shine, the world will see your *"God-Works"* and glorify your God; in the process community is cultivated, the church is successful and God becomes a visible presence in the earth—a true kingdom in motion.

REBUILDING YOUR CITY

So far, we have discussed how the power of community affects every area of life, business and the body of Christ. But what about your city? How can the kingdom of God work in your city? I imagine our cities today as in the days of Nehemiah with the broken down walls of Jerusalem, the ruined city and the oppressed Jewish people. This same heartbreak happens today. There are diseases, terror and rumors of wars. People are crying out for help in cities across the globe, hope is waning, faith is fading fast and chaos is setting in.

Some people say, *"Where is God in all of this?"* Others are in peril and still, many are at a loss for words. The reality is that things will never get better as long as we remain separated and in our own corners of comfort. True enough, this may be the reality in many parts of the world, but it is far from the truth. I say that because **reality is not always seen through the eyes of truth and truth is seldom viewed through the lens of reality.**

Our perception of who we are is directly connected to what we believe when we look into the mirror of our hearts. It often shows us a picture of our faith, our dreams, our passions and the things we love, hate and hope for.

Do you feel a pain for people when you look into the mirror of your heart? Does a desperate desire for change and restoration for the brokenhearted suddenly overwhelm you? After experiencing these symptoms, what do you do about it? Do you sit back in your chair and say, *"Wow! What a catastrophe!"* and simply do nothing? I guess, what I am asking you is this: **What are you going to do about it?** If you do not plan to do anything about what you feel then those feelings are nonessential to you, your life, your purpose, community, city and your world. If this is your perspective, then you are not living but simply existing.

I would like to go far out on a limb and encourage you to not just sit back and exist, but to start living with a purpose to rebuild your city. You are not the only one at fault here; there are millions of other bystanders doing the same thing: basking in their *comfort zones* as their cities fall apart. It may take some time for change to happen but it will also take people who have a willingness to make change happen. Don't just sit back. Get involved in the rebuilding process.

Nehemiah, the king's cupbearer who became the governor of Jerusalem and rebuilt the city walls is our example of how we can rebuild our cities. I encourage you to read the book of Nehemiah. I believe there is a Nehemiah spirit in all of us. You and I also have the same abilities, but what is missing is a burden for change and a willingness to experience discomfort. As a society, we have become far too comfortable at just existing. Living is not for spectators; it is a full contact sport that requires your participation. **We must live it to win it!** Any denial of the above gives death permission to take your place.

What's holding you back? Is it the career, the expensive toys or is it the limiting beliefs? Your perspective on life could have morphed into what's known as the retired entitlement attitude: *"I have worked hard for what I have and it's time for me to enjoy it."* Maybe it's the middleclass mindset at work in you, which says *"I'm just trying to make it."* Even more, you could also have a poverty personality that believes you are too far gone and there is absolutely nothing you can do to change the trajectory of tomorrow. Well, I have news for you. Regardless of your status in society: be it upper-class, middle-class, low or no class at all. Without a city, none of those things will soon matter.

Nehemiah had a secure job in the king's palace. This prestigious responsibility also had its challenges: he was the connection between life and death for the king. As the king's cupbearer any moment could be his last day because the king ate only what Nehemiah first sampled. Still, *he was willing to give up what he did for what he was, a great leader of change.* It took Nehemiah 52 days to complete the great task of rebuilding his country's wall.

The wrong perception is that nothing will happen if you do nothing. That statement is clearly false and misinterpreted. The absolute certainty is that **something always happens even if you decide do nothing, but we can only influence what happens to us when we decide to do something.** The core message here is that things will always happen in life and in your city, *but you get to decide whether they happen to you or for you.*

The scriptures told us that Nehemiah became saddened after he heard about the condition of his people in a faraway land,

Jerusalem. His heart was so broken that his countenance reflected his pain even while serving the king. Brokenness is a function of the heart and these statements are true: "*...for out of the abundance of the heart the mouth speaks*" (Matthew 12: 34b KJV). It had been nearly one hundred years since his people came out of exile and had been in this oppressive, broken and destruct condition.

Nehemiah did not have to do anything because he had a good job, food, shelter and the provisions of the king. But the truth is, even if he did nothing, something still happened to his people and had been for a very long time.

Having prayed to God for wisdom, he told the king the real meaning behind the drastic change in his countenance and he was granted permission to rebuild the city of his people. Today, we remember Nehemiah for his effective approach to *horizontal leadership* and his passion for transforming a nation of Jews. In fact, at each significant stage of Nehemiah's journey to rebuild the walls and restore his people, he asked God to remember his faithful service to the people of Jerusalem: (Nehemiah 5:19; 6:14; 13:14; 13:22; 13:29; 13:31).

So what will it take for you to rebuild your city? It will take a team of dedicated souls with a mind to work. Beyond that, it will also take an individual who has a passion for his city, knows the gifts of his team and how to rally them to accomplish a task so massive that its completion will turn the heart of kings, release the favor of God and bring glory to his name. I encourage you to Go! Gather your team, rebuild your city and take back your community, today.

CHAPTER 7

MISCONCEPTION OF 'SERVICE'

If you are not serving your gift you are hindering progress.

~Andrew E. Guy

Most people, even those of religious sects, misunderstand what it means to serve. If you asked most Christians about their function in the body of Christ, many would proudly tell you that they serve the true and living God. And have been doing so for most of their lives. A familiar comment is *"I'm serving in the army of the Lord."* Unfortunately, this misconception of service to God has been a major source of confusion among many believers for decades.

I have to admit, for many years I used to wonder what it meant to *"Serve God"* in spirit and in truth. I would often see hundreds of people marching to the same *church* band, and singing the same *religious* mantra, *"I'm serving in the army of the Lord."* Now, you have to excuse me but the last time I checked, those who served in the army actually went to a war of some sort; they had extensive training and had to undergo some major transformations. Many even relocated to serve in the war.

When I think of serving in the army, I think about the sacrifice of personal comfort for a greater good: leaving your loved ones behind, giving of your last to those who may never repay, loving those who are unlovable, protecting those who cannot defend themselves and lifting up those who may one day pull you down.

There is a lot of confusion surrounding this concept of what it means to serve God. I had tons of questions but little answers. And like many of you have come to discover, most churches were not in position to explain or to provide needful guidance. Forgive my ignorance, but I used to believe that God had an army of mighty angels, like *"Michael and his boys,"* who fought for us and wreaked havoc on the devil and his misfits. We on the other hand, had only one need to fight and that was the *"Good Fight of Faith."*

So what is all this talk about fighting for the Lord and being in his army? Did I miss something here? Or, did religion sell us a misguided missile that would one day blow up in our religious faces? Can we really serve a God we cannot see? Is this possible? And if we could serve Him, what would be our best service to a Holy God?

SERVING THE INVISIBLE GOD

I hate to be the bearer of bad news, but the facts have been religiously screwed and we are in dire need of a spiritual revelation. To the naked eye, it may seem difficult to see a God you cannot serve and to serve a God you cannot see; at least, that is what I thought. So then, how do we serve God? And why do we have religious people going around saying that they are *"In God's army and that they serve Him only."* What's up with that?

Like many of you, religion has had a major effect on my previous beliefs and it is obvious that there needs to be some form of clarity to finally dissolve this state of confusion. Now, I clearly do not expect everyone to be a *Good Samaritan*, but serving a God that you cannot see may seem oxymoronic, especially when you claim to be living for him. But for those of you who want to develop a deeper relationship with God, I completely understand your dilemma.

I was very confused at first, but because God is not the author of confusion, so I immediately dismissed the thought and sought spiritual clarity.

CLARITY OF SERVICE

How can I serve a God I could not see? At first, I felt like old Nicodemus (who came to Jesus one night) wondering if he could go back into his momma's womb a second time to be born again. I know what you are thinking: *"Say Nic, that's a silly question, my brother! No wonder you came late at night where no one would hear you ask such a dumb question."*

Now many of us would make fun of ole Nic, but can you blame him? After a while of soul-searching, I only hope that you too would develop a *no-holds-barred* mindset when you really need heavenly answers to your earthly questions. I guess ole Nic was not so dumb after all. He was willing to look foolish to gain wisdom and God honors that.

I completely understand how ole Nic must have felt, foolish and inept. I was in the same predicament and a question like serving an invisible God could not be any dumber than going back into the womb a second time. Go figure. I knew it was a dumb question but I still asked anyway. Why? Because I've always believed the foolish things of this world reveal the wisdom of God. I remember saying to God, how could anyone serve you when you have everything? How is this possible? You own everything. *"The earth is the Lord's, and everything in it."* (1 Corinthians 10:26)

I was almost at a level of frustration when the voice said, *"You serve me when you serve people: my image in the earth."* Immediately I knew this was an answer to my prayers. Then clarity came. God is an invisible spirit but we see people every day. *BINGO!* It makes perfect sense, I thought. If we are his creation, his workmanship, the apple of his eye, then whatever we do for the people we see, we actually do the same to the God we can *only* see through them!

> *"No one has ever seen God; but if we love one another, God lives in us and his love is made complete in us"* (1 John 4:12).

"For whoever does not love their brother and sister, whom they have seen, cannot love God, whom they have not seen" (1John 4:20). Jesus also added, *"Anyone who has seen me has seen the Father. How can you say, 'Show us the Father'?"* (John 14:9).

I know what you are thinking and I was right where you are. *"Wait a minute,"* you are saying, *"but he's Jesus, the son, and the reflection of God. How can mere people be just like God in the earth?"* Well, according to 1John 4:17b *"In this world we are like Jesus."* And if the spirit of God that is in Jesus lives in us we are just like him. Got it? I know how you feel. Back then I felt the same way. This is making major sense to me right now and I am completely flabbergasted. So, loving people is the same as loving God and serving people is serving God. Nice! I like it! And I am sticking to it!

SERVING THE IMAGE

I remember Jesus was talking to his disciples and he told them that they had given him bread when he was hungry, water when he was thirsty, shelter when he was homeless and clothing when he was naked, see Matthew 25:35-39. The disciples were in disbelief! They could not see that serving God meant serving the image he created of himself. *"The King will reply, 'Truly I tell you, whatever you did for one of the least of these brothers and sisters of mine, you did for me"* (Matthew 25:40).

It does not matter how minute your actions may seem; *"whatever"* we do to the least of those we see, we actually do it to God, who we cannot see, but who created the least of those we see and serve. *"No one has ever seen God; but if we love one another, God lives in us and his love is made complete in us"* (1 John 4:12). This is powerful! Are you getting this...?

"You serve me when you serve people: my image in the earth."

It is no wonder the Good Samaritan continues to be one of the most talked about biblical examples of how together, we can ALL advance God's kingdom on earth by the way we treat others as service to God. This is how the kingdom works in community. The same way people connect in communities and use their gifts to serve others is identical to organs in the human body coming together to form the organism that sustains life through service.

Every kingdom citizen should be a useful component in his community; then together we are all "used-full" God-images in the sight of God. When you see your sister and brother, you are actually looking at a reflection of God; the truth is, God really sees us as he sees himself. *"As he 'Christ' is, so are we in this world"* (1 John 14:17*b*).

Again, the book of John reminds us that *"Whoever claims to love God yet hates a brother or sister is a liar. For whoever does not love their brother and sister, whom they have seen, cannot love God, whom they have not seen"* (1 John 4:20). Our first service to humanity is love. To love people is to love God. To forgive is to be forgiven. To serve people is to serve God. *"We know that we have passed from death to life, because we love each other"* (1 John 3:14).

FRUITFUL NOT USED-LESS

We are created to bear fruit in our *community-body* and in our area of influence. The lack of fruitfulness results in malfunction and uselessness. Also, if a product's malfunction negatively affects its community or surroundings, it may be cut down and discarded to protect the livelihood of everyone else. Luke 13:7*b* says, *'For three years now I've been coming to look for fruit on this fig tree and haven't found any. Cut it down! Why should it use up the soil?'*

Uselessness affects everyone in a community. Even though the unfaithful servant in the parable used none of his gift it was still "use-full," and so it was taken from him and transferred to a more fertile soil to bear fruit.

In the same way, a car that does not function is "used-less" than the one that works most efficiently. In fact, the *useful* parts from the *"used-less"* car are salvaged (recycled and reused) and put into a "use-full" car to make it even more productive and "full-of-use." Don't just be used, but be full of use. This brings glory to God!

THE ULTIMATE WAY TO SERVE

The ultimate way to serve an invisible God is to serve humans, the (visible) God-images we see every day. You may not know what the creator looks like but he is visible in all his creation. We are created to serve; not to control each other, but rather to "have" control over things, circumstances and events. We are created to have dominion and not to be dominated.

Likewise, every person is designed with specific gifts to be used for making other people better. As we serve, we are establishing, building, promoting and maintaining the Kingdom of God on earth, so that those who are unaware may become aware, believe and discover their "true-selves" and as a result, begin to function with purpose and self-appreciation.

Therefore, ultimate service begins with an appreciation of what you have been entrusted with, your gift and a willingness to share it with the world. It is through this appreciation for what you do (your function) that makes you a person of value so that you can add value to others in your area of expertise or community. Everything you do should add value to the people you serve. So, can anyone add value to others? The answer is an emphatic and a resounding YES! This can be done anywhere, at any time, and to anyone you serve. Here's how…

EVERY GIFT ADDS VALUE

Your gift is the value you are given to enhance others. How you deliver this value to people is called a function. Your passion, ability and the level at which you deliver what you do to improve others is your skill. In other words, a person who is a bricklayer, janitor, doctor, the CEO of a fortune 500 company, or even the leader of a country, possesses an ability to deliver a service that is needed by a group of people in a specific community. Your skillfulness is determined by how well you utilize your gift to serve others.

Take for instance, an automotive technician. This skillful mechanic ensures he does the job right the first time, every time and goes beyond the satisfaction of the customer's need. The janitor who cleans a building also has value. Even though society may consider him/her to be the least on the totem pole of a company's success agenda, he still adds value through his function. How? Because he skillfully and consistently does a prolific job at making sure the floors are spotless and are always in pristine condition every day. This adds value to the building and to those who experience the cleanliness of the environment created by the janitor's efforts.

Likewise, the same can be said about a valuable supervisor who is diligent at serving his staff as he adds value to every worker to bring out the best in each person for the greater good of the company. It may take some time to accomplish this great feat, but over time, the company stands to benefit significantly. A value-centered supervisor seeks to add more to others than take away. Therefore, **your value should not just be visible; those who consume it must experience it.** Real value is more than words; it is an experience.

VALUE DETERMINES WORTH

Your ability to add value to others coupled with the power to influence and create lasting change determines your worth. It can be difficult to determine the value of a person, place or thing without any tangible experience to measure its worth. Though sadly, it is common for society to judge a book by its cover, you should never devalue a thing before you determine its worth.

So what is the difference between value and worth? In simple terms, value is a meaningful experience that promotes growth when extracted from a source, while worth is the power to influence change after value has been added. A person who has attained a billionaire status has acquired significant value and has more than just the *"name"* billionaire. He/she now possesses a power and the ability to significantly influence change in communities and the world at large. Clearly, much value has been added this person, but his worth lies in his ability to influence change. Now how do you suppose this billionaire could demonstrate his worth in the power of community?

Before we answer that, it is important that you see worth as a *"decision-making power"* and not just the accumulation of stuff. In this scenario I want you to know that wealth and worth are analogous because they both possess the inherent power to make decisions that influence change. Now that you have it, let us begin.

Let's imagine this valuable billionaire was watching the nightly news and heard of a war-torn region in some faraway land where hundreds of innocent children were being victimized. As he watched the broadcast, a sense of heartfelt compassion overwhelmed the billionaire and brought him to his knees. After barely regaining his composure, he decided to activate his worth.

His options were vividly clear. Be a spectator of life and simply sit back, do nothing and continue to be a person of value (rich) without worth, or activate his worth to influence a greater change. You see, we all possess this ability but only a few take the necessary actions to declare their worth.

One of the greatest experiences in everyone's life happens the moment people realize they have the power to influence change. It is at this crucial decision point that a person discovers his sense of worth. As a result, at the core of every person's worth is an innate desire to meet the needs of others. God has imparted this great gift to all of us, but the choice is still ours.

With this in mind, the billionaire arrives at a powerful decision point. Next, he made two very important phone calls, one to his wife and the other to his business partner. He then decides to purchase and revamp an old abandoned mattress factory on the south side of his own city and transform it into a shelter for children of war-torn countries. Within ten years the billionaire rescued over fifty-thousand children and transformed their lives for good. Today he is the owner of a multi-billion dollar operation that preserves lives and provides needful hope to victimized children of war.

The life lesson here is this: value creates options, but worth demands that you make decisions to influence change. The moment you decide to activate the power of worth, your value increases exponentially. Who knows, this person may have started out as a *"thousand-aire,"* (if there is such a word) and because of one decision he went from millions to billions. This is the fundamental principle behind the parable of the Good Samaritan. Although the story did not reveal this, I would like to believe that the same thing would have happened for him—his life quadrupled in value and worth from making just one decision to help someone.

In your case, are you increasing your value by declaring your worth? Or, are you simply rich and worthless? Remember, value was given to you for the enhancement of others in your community and the world. I may never have the opportunity to meet you in this life, but rest assured, I am adding value to you as you read these pages. True enough, it may have taken me over six years and endless nights to write this book, but you reading it and extracting its value to expand your growth means more to me than the sleepless nights. My hope is for you to take action once the value is added.

A seed not sown is a harvest postponed, and value not shared is self-worth denied

You are a part of this powerful source that sustains all communities and every person should have access to it. Do not keep value to yourself or death will ensue. Just like the heart in the body, every cell, tissue, organ and organ system has access to the resources it provides through pumping. If the heart suddenly decides to withhold its value and worth, death is inevitable. Therefore, if you are reluctant to share, you have also declined to care. *A seed not sown is a harvest postponed, and value not shared is self-worth denied.*

COMMUNITY AT WORK

There is a power that only exists in community. This power source is the result of all the joint efforts and accumulated forces of the people, who by choice, share their resources and gifts for the overall improvement of everyone. We see this concentrated power of community in every walk of life.

This concept of collective community power is also visible in the construction industry. Next time you are in a major city take a look at the landscape, the architectural designs and building infrastructures. It takes a collective team of community specialists to complete every project that makes a city functional.

Do you recall the wealthy man who exponentially increased his value and worth to *"billionaire"* status by making just one decision to add value to others? Well, he did not do it alone. In his quest to revamp the old abandoned mattress factory, he needed some highly skilled community partners.

You may know them as building specialists. Some did masonry, others were electricians, framers, plumbers, engineers, computer geeks, roofers, brick and tile layers, gardeners and landscapers, interior décor specialists and the list goes on. Together they joined forces, broke down the old factory and rebuilt a brand new shelter that became their haven and a home to thousands of happy children.

Without explaining the nuances of demolishing and reconstructing a new building, the sole purpose of this lengthy list is to demonstrate the power of like-minded people in a shared community and to drive home the message that we all need each other to make us complete.

Likewise, the body is not complete without the heart, legs, arms, eyes, or nose; neither can you breathe without oxygen and all the components of a working respiratory system that collectively sustain life. And so, a community takes all kinds of people to make it a complete support system for everyone. I think you have gotten the message now, but 1 Corinthians 12:16-20 says it best:

"If the whole body were an eye, where would the sense of hearing be? If the whole body were an ear, where would the

sense of smell be? But in fact God has placed the parts in the body, every one of them, just as he wanted them to be. If they were all one part, where would the body be? As it is, there are many parts, but one body. And if the ear should say, "Because I am not an eye, I do not belong to the body," it would not for that reason stop being part of the body."

We are all vital parts of a kingdom design that makes up the anatomical body of a community. Every person on earth is a valuable part of society and does play an intricate role in their community. In the "community-body", nothing is vestigial. Every part is necessary and has a value and a worth to influence positive change. *"So we, who are many, are one body in Christ, and individually members one of another"* (Romans. 12:5).

This is the nature of the kingdom of God in motion. It is service driven, gift-centered and value focused to improve worth.

WHAT DOES COMMUNITY MEAN TO YOU?

I want you to think about this as we journey through our next discussion about the purpose of community.

CHAPTER 8

COMMUNITY MEETS A NEED

It is because we are spirit beings
that we need community.
~Andrew E. Guy

At the core of every community is the desire to experience positive social interactions. This need for social interaction can only be met by other people in a community. It is for this specific reason that things do not always fill the gap we experience during isolation. Through sickness or even in death, *people are the medicine to our social needs but it is God who writes the prescription.*

It is not because we are religious that we need religion,
but it is because we are spirit beings
that we need community.

However, beyond the surface of social interactions there is a deeper need that is not always detected by the naked eye. This invisible need is not associated with religion because religion is an orchestrated controlled practice that neither sustains nor empowers the human spirit, but rather, repels and destroys the concept of community.

It is not for the love of things, comfort, security or access to resources that we need community—it is because we need each other. We don't just need each other to "hang out with". We need to connect in ways that create meaning.

This significant human need involves a shared community of like-minded people who jointly use their specialized gifts to support each other. Just like attaining homeostasis in the human anatomy (the perfect replica of a community) this mutual support of each other creates the balance we experience called *oneness*. This is why the most valuable resource on planet earth is not things; it is people.

USEFULNESS IN COMMUNITY

Any profession you can think of has a built-in service component for adding value to people in a specific community. For example, teachers preserve the future by adding value to their students. The mechanic adds value to his customer by making sure that the vehicle is safe to drive. We are components and building blocks of supernatural greatness for *use-full-ness*.

The term "usefulness" in this context simply means ones' ability to use your area of giftedness to produce an expected end or bear fruit. An apple tree will only bear apples, nothing else; likewise, an orange, cherry, or even a monkey, will only reproduce after its own kind.

Any creation that does not fulfill its created purpose (to bear fruit and add value) based on the manufacturer's specifications, is said to malfunction and becomes useless. Note, *"useless"* does not always mean discarded and without value; here, it simply means, *"Used-Less"* or has little use in terms of functionality and productivity.

The parable of the talents demonstrates the perfect analogy of the term "usefulness." According to Matthew 25:18, three different talents were issued but only one was taken away from the servant who did not bear fruit. Jesus told this parable in order to paint the picture of usefulness. He told his disciples that a certain master departed from his home, and gave his three servants three sets of talents based on their specific abilities and skillfulness: one got five, the other two and another, one.

> *"Fruitfulness and usefulness are synonymous but they require faithfulness"*

Unlike the other two servants who bore fruit and multiplied their talents with a return on the master's investment, the one whom the master had entrusted with only one talent malfunctioned and was deemed useless, unproductive and unprofitable. Although *"he"* was useless his talent was still "useful, and it was taken from him and given to the more profitable servant who was "full-of-use."

Fruitfulness and usefulness are synonymous and they require faithfulness. Here we see a servant who malfunctioned and became useless, unproductive and unprofitable. Unfaithfulness is the root cause of many human malfunctions. Being faithful in a few things, even one talent, will make us ruler over much more. In the world of consumer goods and services, people quickly lose faith in a product when it malfunctions. Furthermore, if a particular product (or function) is known to have recurring failures, its value will depreciate significantly because it lacks the ability to add value to those who consume it.

Who knows why the *"used-less"* servant in the parable did not put his talent to good use; even though the scriptures said his motive for not multiplying his master's talent was because of fear and disobedience.

"I knew that you are a hard man, harvesting where you have not sown and gathering where you have not scattered seed. So I was afraid and went out and hid your talent in the ground. See, here is what belongs to you" (Matthew 25:24).

I believe **unfaithfulness breeds uselessness**. The opposite is true that faith is the ability to believe that we are wired (supernaturally designed) to do what we were created to do (function with purpose and add value to others); while fear is the complete opposite or a belief that we are incapable of doing what we are designed to do, so we resolve to do nothing.

FAITHFULNESS LEADS TO RULER-SHIP

Bearing fruit is a process that involves a person's ability to add lasting value to people so they, in turn, can add value to others.

We are chosen and mandated to not only bear fruit but much fruit. John 15:16a says, *"You did not choose me but I chose you, and appointed you that you would go and bear fruit, and that your fruit would remain."* In short, we are all valuable instruments of divine purpose and spiritually designed to inhabit the earth and bear fruit.

Faithfulness leads to ruler-ship, advancement and increased promotion. At the end of life, our goal is never to get a sparkling trophy or a retirement clock to sit back in our lounge chairs and watch our time slip by, but to be called *"good and faithful servant"* of the gifts or talents we have been entrusted with. The skilled mechanic gets more customers because he does an outstanding job every time for each customer.

Likewise, the venture capitalist is rewarded when the wise investor greatly improves the return on his investments. Equally, faithful parents are rewarded with a 'restful' old age and receive great honor for their commitment to raising children with sound principles and honorable character.

It does not matter what the talent or gift is (a janitor, mechanic, teacher, doctor, lawyer or homemaker); just use it to the glory of God to serve others in your community, and be diligent and faithful to the end. *"Well done, good and faithful servant! You have been faithful with a few things; I will put you in charge of many things. Come and share your master's happiness!"* (Matthew 25:21).

We are products of purpose with Supernatural Greatness and Usefulness

---

Remember, every person is designed with a specific gift to be used for making others better by establishing, building, promoting and maintaining the Kingdom of God on earth, so that those who are unaware may become aware, believe and discover their "true-selves" and begin to function with purpose. Being fruitful is the process of producing a result based on the manufacturer's specifications, while usefulness is the ability of a product to add value and meet a need.

More specifically, the created fruit or end product must be usable by those who consume it. Malfunction occurs if what you create does not fulfill its intended purpose, it is therefore useless. Also note, useless does not always mean discarded and without value; although it can, it simply means, "Used-Less" or has little use in terms of functionality.

Being faithful to our gift means we place a high value on it. This is why covetousness goes against Kingdom principles. Each gift is specific to each person based on his or her individual potential and abilities. Abandoning your gift for someone else's compromises your ability to use your gift and causes malfunction in the body. Willful abandonment of your gift negatively affects your community. Your purpose for living becomes an unknown quest of trials and error, and a costly experiment called effort—a wasted life. One of the keys to being faithful to your gift is to want what you have and to put to good use what you've been entrusted with.

GIFTS ARE SPECIFIC TO PURPOSE

Everyone was created to perform a specific function, at a specific time, for a specific purpose, in a specific area of giftedness, for a specific generation. Nothing will happen if you fail to do your part. An unfulfilled purpose is a result of malfunction. Your gift is specific to you and you alone. Therefore, no one can do what you were created to do and you can never be replaced. Life becomes meaningful and purpose driven when you do what you do like an original that can neither be copied nor be replaced. You are necessary. Say out loud five times, *"I AM NECESSARY IN THE KINGDOM OF GOD AND IN MY COMMUNITY."*

Like a fingerprint, no two are identical, but each has a different set of identities that separate one from the other. You are the only one of your type and skill-set; there is no other coming back after you are gone. Therefore, it is vital that you know your purpose for living, utilize your gift and use it to serve the body of Christ and your community.

If you fail to carry out your function, an area of the kingdom suffers, community collapses and the will of God for your life is unfulfilled. Similarly, if the alternator in a car fails to generate enough power to supply the engine, the car cannot fulfill its functional purpose to "drive" and as a result, becomes a hindrance instead of a productive aid to make transporting easier.

> **"You were created for a purpose with an expected end in mind"**

Likewise, if the heart fails to fulfill its functional purpose of "pumping" blood in order to distribute nutrients and oxygen to the body, cells, then the body and all its systems will fail to fulfill their purpose of "living." As a result, purpose for living is cancelled and death occurs. Are you getting this?

Everyone serves a divine purpose when you function. Each person has a built-in set of unique skills and abilities that validate their existence and play a vital role in a global community called the kingdom of God. I want you to discover who you are and what you were created to do, your function.

Every part in a system is important; if one component fails, the system will malfunction. This is why it is important for each person to take ownership of his gift, develop it and then use it for the glory of God. The Creator gets no glory in failure and malfunction. One of the surest ways to malfunction is to want what someone else has. This a clear sign of neglecting your role and function. Covetousness robs you of your victory and denies God of his glory.

The gift that each person receives is specific to his or her ability; just like King David used his sling and a stone instead of King Saul's sword and shield. Therefore, your success is guaranteed when you operate in your area of expertise and giftedness. David would have failed miserably, his team would have been annihilated and disgraced by Goliath had he used King Saul's armor and sword. But he was victorious when he used his skill with a sling and a stone that was backed by the power of his God.

A neglected gift negatively affects the livelihood of any community it was designed to serve the same way a bad kidney jeopardizes the entire immune system of the body and renders it prone to infection. The body relies heavily on every component functioning optimally. Should one fail, immunity is compromised and the body becomes weakened as deadly viruses attack the body's vital organs and threaten its survival.

Since every joint supplieth, your gift was designed to sustain and protect you, your family, your community and the kingdom at large. When you desire another person's gift, you are simply saying that your gift is useless and without value, while the other person's gift is better and you should have it instead. Neglecting your gift weakens the kingdom the same way the body is defenseless without its supportive members. 1 Corinthians 12:15-26, says:

> *"Now if the foot should say, "Because I am not a hand, I do not belong to the body...And if the ear should say, "Because I am not an eye, I do not belong to the body...If the whole body were an eye, where would the sense of hearing be...If one part suffers, every part suffers with it; if one part is honored, every part rejoices with it."*

You were specifically created to fulfill a specific function in your generation. If you are faithful in your area of giftedness and use it to build and improve others, the giver of all gifts will promote you and make you ruler over much more. Remember, faithfulness leads to promotion and your gift is designed to take you before kings and nations.

What about you? Are you being faithful with your gifts, talents, skills and abilities? It is never too late; you can start today. Remember, *"YOU ARE NECESSARY IN THE KINGDOM OF GOD, IN YOUR COMMUNITY AND IN THE WORLD."*

YOU ARE SALT AND LIGHT

You are the salt and light of the world. I want you to think of the world as a small community that is in peril and utter darkness, and your gift and function allows you to preserve others and add light to this community. The world needs your salt and light.

The *name* salt has little use without its identity, the property of saltiness. In essence, one is a name and the other is a function that has a chemical property to preserve. Sodium Chloride, (NaCl) is the chemical denotation used to describe the compound, salt. The importance of this illustration is not to highlight the name, but rather, the function of this substance.

In Matthew 5:13-16, after Jesus finished his *"Sermon on the Mount,"* he later told the disciples and those gathered, about the concept of salt and light. Kingdom citizens must know that they have a property of "saltiness" that preserves the earth. Notice that "saltiness" refers to a function, which is the chemical identity of the substance and it's ability to preserve something that is perishable.

Again, Jesus reminds them that having the name *"salt"* means nothing if the salt has lost its (function) *"saltiness."* Once the substance loses its chemical function or power (*"saltiness"*) it is considered useless and should only be trampled under your feet.

"You are the light of the world," Jesus added, *"A city on a hill."* Why would he use these two examples to explain this concept of your value in the kingdom? You are the city that sustains life and your location is vital to those who seek your help. You must be visible, not hidden, on a hill where you can be seen. A lighthouse is visible to any oceangoing vessel in its vicinity. It must be visible not hidden and so should you.

> *"There's great power in knowing your value and owning your function"*

Jesus also said, *"Let your light shine "before" men, that they may "see" your good deeds and praise the Father in heaven."* While "saltiness" has a specific function and a location, light also has a specific function. There is a major difference between earth and the world; one is a physical location and the other is a system. So while God's intention is to preserve a location (earth) for his kingdom, He also requires a system (the world) that represents his presence in that location. The light is God's spirit, which works through us to light up a dark and sinful world (a system) and to bring clarity to those who are lost.

It is very rare to see "good news" reported in the media. Why? Because to a great extent the "world," system is fueled by darkness and fear. Negative news breeds fear, anxiety and confusion. Media companies are built on such propaganda. Ratings and internet clicks are fueled by negativity because the purpose of promoting evil is to increase scarcity and inflict fear. Where fear is present faith is absent. Where there is no hope and revelation, faith is lost and the people throw off restraint and crime and violence ensue. Emphasis added. (See Proverbs 29:18).

You are the only hope that the "world" has. **You are the light, and when you shine, confusion is lost and wisdom is found, fear disappears, faith appears, hate is denounced and love abounds.** Could you imagine a world where "good news" was popular and bad news had no significance? Just imagine, a large percent of the world would be unemployed because there would be nothing bad to report, no crime to fight and weapons of mass destruction would be pointless. There would be no need for spying satellites or chemical warfare.

This is why you must shine, and shine bright enough for the systems of the dark "world" to see. And do not stop there either. Your location is paramount to your ability to illuminate and shine. You must not only shine, you must be visible. Your function is a necessary part of every community. Do not lose your "saltiness" and do not cease to shine!

A REALLY "USED-FULL" SHOW

There's something amazing about shining your light for the world to see, that makes usefulness a practical part of everyday life. When my sons were younger, one of our favorite pastimes was to watch episodes of *Thomas the Tank Engine and Friends*.

The *Island of Sodor* is a great example of a kingdom community in action. Similar to the anatomy of the human body having many parts, *Sodor* requires full participation from all the engines to make the island a special place for visitors to keep coming back year after year. The island has a diversified array of every possible types of engine you could imagine, and there's even a helicopter named *Harold,* my favorite.

The engines do everything from digging quarries to shunting and hauling freight. Aside from all the daily activities that the engines are asked to do, being a useful "*USED-FULL*" engine is at the top of their goal. Despite their function, paint color, size or speed, every engine on *Sodor Island* aims to impress the head of the railway, *Sir Topham Hatt,* by doing just that—being really "*USED-FULL*".

Being "*USED-FULL*" is another way of being faithful in your function as you use your gift to serve others in the body of your "*Sodor*" community. Of course, you may not be an engine on an island, but I encourage you to bloom where you are planted and *serve where you are sown*. Everything you see is temporal and is subject to change but you are designed to bring about a greater change in others.

So, never despise your current location or temporary setbacks; none of this is coincidental. Just like Esther of the bible, who became a reigning queen and saved her people from total annihilation, you too may have been called for such a time as this to transform your community as you add value to others. We are organs of the body of Christ who are always on a community assignment.

APPRECIATE WHO YOU ARE

Before anyone can be useful and serve well, he must first accept his gift and want what he has. Therefore, one of the keys to sustaining the power of any community is taking ownership of your gift and the value you add to others. "*…If the whole body were an eye, where would the sense of hearing be?*" (1 Corinthians 12:17*b*)

It is incumbent upon you to want what you have because you did not have to get it. This is why covetousness (to desire the gifts of others instead of what you have) is contrary to you fulfilling your purpose and serving others. Why? Because everyone is gifted differently. You may not be able to handle or carry the load that someone else carries; moreover, your area of expertise may grossly differ from the people you were designed to serve. Just imagine if the heart was the leg and the eye were the kneecap? Do you see how quickly chaos can arise?

The power of community is comprised of specialized components that know their value and own their function. Let's say you were a gifted four-cylinder car who does an excellent job pulling a four-by-six (4x6) U-Haul trailer to transport food and wares for the local homeless shelter ministry. You have been doing this seemingly small insignificant job for the past thirty years, then, suddenly the director of the homeless shelter decides to expand the shelter services to five additional locations. You also noticed that the workload has increased tremendously and more equipment would be needed.

Two weeks into the shelter's expansion and just moments before you made your last delivery of the day, you noticed a huge tractor-trailer steadily humming up the road to the shelter's loading dock. To your surprise, this new trailer will be taking over ninety-five percent of the workload! Suddenly, you begin to dread what might happen to your value and your thirty years of usefulness. "Will they replace me?" You thought. "Maybe it would have been better if "I" were a large tractor-trailer that could carry more and do more, then perhaps the director might decide to keep me."

Many of us fall frequently into the trap of devaluing ourselves in light of someone else's gift. We want what they have instead of what we had. Notice I stated, "*We had.*" It is crucial for you to understand that, the moment you desire what others have you relinquish your rights to what you have. You are no longer in the position to add value to your gift or to others. Do not do that. Just be you and be faithful in a few things. *In a world where you can be just about anything under the sun...don't—just be you!* A community is only as powerful as the value of each supporting component. Regardless of your job, be it insignificant or grand, do it with all your heart. Do not desire to do the job of a truck. This leads to burnout and self-destruction. The role you play in your community is vital to the overall success of everyone you serve and those attached to them.

There's absolutely nothing wrong with having a desire to do greater things, but let it be in your own scope of practice and not of others. You may not be able to handle the workload of a semi-tractor-trailer truck. But if you are faithful in your area of giftedness and use it to build and improve others, the giver of all gifts will promote you and make you ruler over much more, even greater than those who are stronger and more *"tractor"* than you.

> *"You are too unique to be overlooked and far too amazing to be forgotten—just be you"*

The takeaway is simply this, every community has needs but in order for you to meet the needs of others you must be faithful to your gift, appreciate who you are and just be you.

CONNECTION IS THE KEY TO ACCESSING THE HIDDEN TREASURES IN PEOPLE.
~Andrew E. Guy

PART III

MAKING COMMUNITY WORK: CONNECTION IS KEY

CHAPTER 9

THE TECHNOLOGY ANALOGY
Establishing True Kingdom Connection

Since we live in a world where the use of computers have become a third hand or third leg to millions of people world-wide, I thought it would be fitting to use a technological approach with computers and the internet to illustrate this concept of the Kingdom of God in motion as it relates to community.

I want to establish that a kingdom connection is made possible through a personal relationship with your Creator through Jesus Christ. *You do not have to do good works to impress God. You do not need a religion to reach Him.* Good works are not a requirement; however, they are a result of the presence of his Spirit. It is vital that each person has the hardware (personal Wi-FI of faith) that allows him/her to connect. Therefore, I encourage you to get connected.

In a diverse community, the reason each person needs to be connected is to share resources and receive divine revelations to improve function as we share the message of the kingdom with others. We all need this connection, the sooner the better. Many attempt to connect for various reasons. Some connect to give, while others connect to receive. In other words, no one person has everything he/she needs to live effectively. You need people and you need community, as computers need each other on the World Wide Web. Even though we are fully equipped with unlimited resources, we still need added information (wisdom to know how to use the resources we have) and guidance from others to be fully optimized to make us more functionally relevant in our generation.

Your computer must be connected to access the web's abundant resources

This is what Jesus was talking about when He said, *"I come to give you life, and more abundantly..."* He came to prepare your spiritual-systems (your minds) for optimal functioning. Jesus came to remove the "viruses and malwares" from your hard drives, to reformat your (your minds) and tune-up your WI-FI so you may have optimal connection to receive maximum downloads for your spirit-being. He then left so that the connector (the Holy Spirit) would come to help make the connection between you, the Kingdom and the King (Jesus).

You will know that you have maximum connection with God when you have all your signal bars. Your connectivity is drastically reduced when your bars are low. My question to you is this: ***Are you connected? And is your connection signal***

strong? Through this divine connection, you and I are able to replicate the Kingdom of God on earth...Let God's will (His word) be done on earth (replicated) just like it is in heaven."

Once you have a strong connection, you can download all that God has for you. Your download can be anything you need. Sometimes it may be information you need to share with others that will help motivate, encourage and build them up. It could also be an antivirus that you may require to defend yourself (your spiritual system) from a self-destructive mindset.

There's a level of maturity that believers must advance to in order for them to have kingdom influence in every area of life. Paul encouraged us in Romans 12:2 and in Hebrews 5:14 to be transformed by the renewing of our minds by revelations and through the practice of the word that brings about maturity (skillful use) and not from the direct downloads alone.

HINDRANCES TO KINGDOM CONNECTIVITY

Sometimes a visible signal doesn't always mean you are connected to the source. In the same way, you may be praying very hard to get through to God and nothing happens. Sometimes you may have a strong signal (five bars or more to be exact) but you lack the connectivity due to a wrong password or a bad virus.

In this case, you could be saying *all the right words* and quoting them directly from the word of God (or pressing the right letters on your keyboard) but still not connecting optimally.

A BAD PASSWORD

Lack of faith is one of the primary factors that limits our connection to heaven's web. *"So why would someone need to have a password to access the spiritual web? I thought you said all I needed is the connection and a personal Wi-Fi?"* True enough, but you should know that you are making a divine connection to a secured network and a private IP address, which requires a well-encrypted password called faith.

In other words, you may have the right equipment but can still be denied connection due to a bad password like unbelief. So, typing your password and pressing ENTER is the same thing as saying or repeating something directly from God's word, like *"All things work together for my good..."* but without faith your access will be denied. What do you say when things fall apart? Do you continue believing or do you use a different password? If so, you will be denied.

A BAD VIRUS

An unsecured network is similar to religion. You never know what is behind the firewall until you get in. And once you connect to a bad network, there is nothing good on the other side. Here is a clue: on the other side is everything that affects your optimal functioning, your connectivity and your ability to utilize the right operating system (OS) to bring glory to God.

By the way, your "OS" is simply a term used to describe any software or the platform that allows your physical computer (the hardware) to function. Some examples are Microsoft Windows for PC's and OS X Mavericks (version 10.9) for Apple's Macintosh computers.

You can become infected with religious doctrines in the form of bad viruses that corrupt and cripple your system and cause you to malfunction. Sometimes it can take a lot of effort, time and, unfortunately, the loss of vital data for your system to be restored back to normal after a viral or malware attack of the enemy. And since we are speaking in computer terms, your mind is like the hard drive on a computer system. It is difficult to rid your system of mental malwares and bad viruses once it becomes infected. Most times the "computer doctor" or technician will reprogramme or reformat your hard drive.

This means wiping your system clean of all software you previously installed and starting you from scratch. In the same way, we too need to be spiritually reformatted, *(transformed by the reformatting of our minds)* to experience abundant living. *"But be ye transformed by the renewing of your mind, that ye may prove what is that good, and acceptable, and perfect, will of God."* (Romans 12:2 KJV)

In order to avoid being disconnected from your spiritual network, you must know, practice and keep your password safe and your system free from viruses like religious indoctrinations that paralyze the system of your mind.

HEAVEN'S SERVER

God is infinite in ALL His ways and ever accessible to whoever believes. Anyone can connect to obtain whatever resource he/she needs. In the kingdom of God, everyone has what I call, a built-in Wi-Fi that directly connects him to God, the ultimate source of all things. Unlike hardwired-religion, the kingdom of God gives you the flexibility to be anywhere in the world and still be connected to the God-source by faith. No medium is required only a personal WI-FI, your faith-centered relationship with the ultimate source.

The mobile or WI-FI (faith) allows each device or person to connect to the kingdom's web resource anywhere, so long as your "personal WI-FI" signal of faith is available, you can connect. It is faith that makes all things possible and keeps you connected to the source. **Without "Wi-Fi" it is impossible to "connect to the source" or please God.** Because this connectivity is solely based on faith and having a personal relationship with the Creator, the individual no longer needs a religious-medium to have direct access to heaven's web resources. They can go boldly to the throne of grace and make their requests known.

Your connectedness with heaven's server allows you to receive unlimited downloads directly from God himself. Y*ou should not live by the evening news or social media at all, but by every download that comes directly from the server of God.* He empowers you to live the abundant life and to overcome hard times.

CONNECTION IS KEY

I remember one Friday afternoon my youngest sister and I went to drop her daughter to her first day of campus residency and life as a new university nursing student. This was her baby, her only child. My sister was both excited and a little nervous at the same time because this was a big day for both of them and she wanted it to go really well. My sister did everything to make sure her *"Future Nurse Practitioner"* had everything she needed to be successful.

On the way, she decided to stop and pick up a few extra things for her daughter. (Talk about being a model mother. She's a role model for single mothers out there and I'm so proud of her). After gathering the extra items, we got in the car and proceeded to leave, but the car would not start. Everything went dead. There was complete silence. My Sis' started to panic; this was a big day for her and her daughter and she wanted it to go as smoothly as possible.

She tried turning the key with great hopes that the car would give her the gift of Christmas and just, START! But nothing would give. She tried everything and still, nothing. I love my Sis' and would do anything for her. And after watching her frustration mounting, I jumped in to help.

I tried starting the car a few times and got the same result. As a certified science teacher, we are trained to always question the obvious and use the problem solving method where possible. I popped the hood and checked to see if there were any loose wires that had become disconnected or if there were any breakages in electrical continuity. For several minutes I looked diligently and found nothing. Between trying to keep her calm, monitoring our check-in time, reassuring my niece all will be well, and finding a solution, my brain kicked into solution ultra-mode.

Time was winding down so I checked the car's manual for troubleshooting clues. After coming up short again I started asking myself a few diagnostic questions, like, "W*hat does a* *car need to start?* Well, that's a no-brainer! *POWER!* IT NEEDS POWER! Okay then, I thought. Now what gives the car *POWER?* Well, I thought, the alternator charges the battery while driving, and so the car will have enough *POWER* (a fully charged battery) to restart. *It needs power!*

I started saying to myself. "*It needs power. It needs power. It... needs...power!*" I lifted the hood up and decided to hunt down someone with jumper cables to give me a "boost". After begging several people in the parking lot for a boost, they all turned me down and again I went back under the hood and continued my nosing around. I asked my sister to get back into the car and *just follow a few simple instructions*; for example, turn the key and then tell me what you see. Any lights? I asked her. She said, No! She sounded very disappointed.

After coming up with a bunch of NO's, I thought of one last resort; removing the battery terminals to check for corrosion. Then, BANG! There was my answer. I knew the problem had something to do with the power supply but I just could not put my finger on it. It turns out; my finger was in fact dead on both the problem and the solution. The moment I shifted the positive terminal it slid right off in my hand! I also checked the negative and the same thing happened! Neither of them had been securely connected to the battery posts. Both were extremely loose and caused the power shortage.

I quickly looked up and at the same time, slammed my head into the under hood of the car. The pain I felt was nothing in comparison to the joy of finally uncovering the culprit to my sister's delight. *A disconnection in the power supply prevented the car from starting.*

THE TECHNOLOGY ANALOGY

I called out to her from underneath the hood of the car and asked her to do me one last favor: look at the dashboard and tell me what you see. Any lights? I asked her, as I touched the battery terminal posts (negative and positive) with the wires. YES! YES! She said as her eyes widened and lit up like fireworks in the sky at a theme park. What did you do? She asked. I said you had lost connectivity. You had no connection to the POWER SOURCE that enables your car to start and then drive. So having a good connection saved the day.

You see, without connection, you have nothing and the car will remain powerless, even though it has all the capabilities of driving. No connection equals No POWER! You must be connected to the source. My sister was so ecstatic. She quickly got on her cell phone and called mom: *"He did it! He did it! Andrew fixed the car!"* she said. Even though I was glad to assist in any way I could, it never dawned on me to gloat in the praise she gave me; however, I took a simple life lesson from our ordeal.

We all have the power to start, serve and grow, but without the proper connection and the right source, we are powerless. Until we connect to the power source that invigorates, encourages, inspires, motivates and transforms us, we are simply a cold engine block sitting there waiting to get started. The sad thing is, most of us live our lives sitting and never get started because we were never connected to that source of power in the first place. I encourage you to get connected today and *START* your engines to begin your journey to destiny.

THE MOST POWERFUL CONNECTION

The most powerful connection you can ever make is with Jehovah God your Creator. Start today and make the greatest connection of your life. Romans 10:9-10 says, *"...if thou shalt confess with thy mouth Jesus `as' Lord, and shalt believe in thy heart that God raised him from the dead, thou shalt be saved...for with the heart man believeth unto righteousness; and with the mouth confession is made unto salvation."* Simply say these words and believe them with all your heart:

"Dear King, I have malfunctioned and fallen short of your glory; forgive me! From this moment forward, I want to reign with you and function as a citizen in your kingdom. I confess with my mouth that Jesus is Lord, and I believe that you, God, raised him from the dead. Please fill me with your Holy Spirit right now. In Jesus' name. Amen."

God is accessible to anyone who wants to connect. Notice, you did not have to be in a church building or at an altar to connect with God through Jesus Christ. I would, however, recommend that you become part of a church body of believers where you can connect to the kingdom community and serve your gift. You do not need a religion to connect with your God; you need a relationship by faith.

THE CONNECTION ACT

Everything in the Kingdom of God is interconnected and our connection was designed to influence the world. Jesus is the connector, the Holy Spirit makes the connection but it is the power of God (Emmanuel) that works in and through us.

In order for God to work through us, we must understand that he has a master plan for humanity, one that I call the *"Kingdom Act."* His mandate was for all to be saved and none left behind. Similar to the *No Child Left Behind* (NCLB) Act, by former United States President, George W. Bush.

Jesus came to seek and find the lost, restore the broken and to establish His Act, known as the *No Soul Left Behind* (NSLB) Act. Jesus was so adamant about saving the lost that he was willing to leave what he had for what he wanted: to populate the earth realm with species after HIS own kind; to dominate the earth and inoculate it with the mindset of the kingdom, and to collectively rule and dominate the world systems by teaming up with other like-minded citizens to expand the kingdom of God on earth.

CONNECT TO LIVE

CONNECTION IS THE KEY to accomplishing any task in life, especially if it has anything to do with living things. The body is made of trillions of small structures called cells. Specific cells then come together to form tissues and organs, and groups of organs assemble to form a much larger system known as an organ system. These organ systems further connect to make up an interactively interdependent more complex system called an organism. This created organism, a living entity, is given a divine purpose and a function for its existence. Everything created has with it a structure and a function. And purpose is established when the created organism operates in the manner in which it was designed to function.

The body, also known as a living entity, is given life, a purpose and an assignment to fulfill within its lifespan. The fulfillment of this assignment is accomplished by connecting with other similar organisms in a community to serve. We are a community of parts designed to serve each other. But before this can happen, there must first be a connection. Likewise, the body is made up of many parts that serve the entire body to create and sustain life. Because every member is vital to the overall success of the body, no one organism is more important than the other. Therefore, there is nothing vestigial (without purpose or useless) in the anatomy of the kingdom body we call a community.

All are significant to the fulfillment of everyone's assignment. In other words, the same way that the body is interconnected and each organ works diligently to support the other to create the ideal internal balance called homeostasis, each of us must connect and serve our gifts to assist the other in order to fulfil the ultimate assignment of each organism. Collectively, we are an interdependently interconnected organism.

If one organism is successful, all are successful. If one organ fails, the entire body is compromised and becomes susceptible to extinction. It is not always the *"strongest that survives,"* but together we live and divided we die. We are the sum total of each of our potential greatness. Like a pair of hands, each one washes the other (through lathering and rinsing) as they both become clean. In an interconnected community, each person strengthens the other, while everyone becomes infinitely stronger.

I recently saw a slogan that said, *"Our product is steel, but our strength is people."* In the same way, our source is God and our combined forces are the strength of the foundation that creates communities.

CONNECT AND SERVE

Connection is the key to the Kingdom function. ***Where there is a disconnect, there's no meaning, no function and no purpose for existing.*** If the heart does not connect to the upper and lower vena cava, (the main passageways that transport blood from the heart to the upper and lower body) it would have no reason to pump. Likewise, if the legs do not connect to your body, they would have no purpose to ambulate or walk; the body would become immobile. And without assistance, you would become permanently fixed to one place, forever.

Therefore, the body would have no reason to be alive—death is a result. Similar to the analogy Jesus made in *John 15:1-6*, a cluster of grapes that is removed from the vine can no longer receive nutrients from the vine, neither can it get any sweeter—death is its plight. It must be connected to receive nutrients.

If you are searching for a reason to live effectively and with purpose, you must first connect to God, then reach out to be connected in the body of your community and use your giftedness to serve others and expand God's kingdom here on earth. The reason why people move from one community to another is because they feel disconnected; hence, they have no reason to stay.

The same experience is felt for those who leave jobs or abandon their families. They disconnect themselves from the mission and vision of the family or company because they can no longer find a reason to stick around. Connection is key in God's Kingdom.

In order to activate the engine and extract the power-of-drive that is trapped within its pistons, you must have the right key.

~ Andrew E. Guy

CHAPTER 10

KINGDOM CONNECTIVITY
"Your Personal Wi-Fi"

Religion restricts, cripples and oppresses its participants, while the kingdom of God permits freedom, enablement and connectedness for a greater purpose. Unlike religion, the kingdom of God is a system of functions based on connectivity through meaningful and intentional relationships. But in order for you to effectively relate to others, each person must be connected to a source that provides the necessary resources he/she needs to carry out a specific function to build up the body within the community one is in.

Ideally, the body is built-up, supported and maintained when each person shares his gift (resource) to serve others. Like organs of the body (brain, heart, lungs, muscles, kidneys, spleen, etc.), so is everyone, a significantly vital partner in the kingdom community. It doesn't matter what your area of specialty is (preacher, teacher, farmer, banker, lawyer, scientist, parent, mechanic, doctor or judge), do it with all your heart as unto God.

As you do your part with precision and grace, encourage others to do the same or even better. *"Therefore encourage one another and build each other up...hold them in the highest regard in love because of their work"* (1 Thessalonians 5:11-13 KJV). It is this divine relationship and connectedness to the source which provides us a direct connection to all the resources we need to live effectively. The lack of connection leads to malfunction, death and unexpected extinction.

So why is connectivity a vital part of your survival in any community? Simple; *we connect so we can serve better; we serve better when we function optimally; we function optimally when we are connected to our God to receive direct downloads onto our spiritual hard drives that bring divine revelations to make you a better servant of your gifts.* Whew! I know that was a big chunk to swallow, but if you would hang in there with me, I will bring more clarity to you as it relates to connectivity.

THE KINGDOM WEB

The kingdom can also be seen as one connected human-web. Let us use computers and the web to help you make this virtual connection. We will assume that almost everyone has a computer or at least, has access to one. Now imagine that there is a central hub or server, which stores the critical information that all computers need in order to function correctly. Next, think of people in this divine web-connection the same way you would think of connected computers on the *World Wide Web*, the Internet.

If each individual were to be compared to a personal computer (laptop, desktop, tablet, Apple, Windows or Android device) that connects to a web server or satellite to access and share resources, then there are many reasons why people, like computers, connect with each other. They would do this to access required information in the form of hardware or software (*"geeks"* know these as updates, plugins, drivers, patches, antivirus defense, etc.) to make them function more productively and efficiently.

But most importantly, why so great a need for us to connect? *Answer:* everyone has what the next person needs, and no *"ONE"* person has everything s/he requires to live a fulfilled life. This is why connection is key: We connect so we can serve better; we serve better when we function optimally; we function optimally when we are connected to a source to receive supernatural downloads to our hard drives that bring divine revelations or how-to instructions so we can better relate.

Question: Could you imagine what the world would be like if the internet and computers could not connect and share? *Answer*: there would be neither web nor virtual social communities, and Mark Zuckerberg of Facebook would be *"virtually"* unheard of. Today through virtual connections the internet serves more than half the world's population. And according to an *October 2014* online article in The *Washington Post, "Almost as many people use Facebook as live in the entire country of China."* [1] There are over 1.35 billion users connected on Facebook. That's a staggering 20 percent of the world's population who log onto Facebook alone, once a month.[2] Wow!

Now go with me a little further back to the pre-internet days, and even long before cell phones and mobile communication devices. What do you see? There were less people connecting, less availability of information, fewer virtual relationships, and of course, fewer people walking around with their eyes glued to a mobile device and typing with their thumbs. Even our languages have changed in order to accommodate this new means of communication: *LOL, WWJD, OMG,* and all because of the internet and the propensity of people to create shortcuts to connect.

Are you starting to get the picture now? The things that you are now able to do today were only an imaginative myth back then. Technology has made it possible for the world to connect by just the click of a button. And get this, my sixty-five year old mother, who had less than a tenth grade education now has a cell phone and a tablet and is more tech savvy than a monkey with a ripe banana. Go figure. *LOL!* For most people, their mobile devices are like a second pair of appendages (legs and hands) that keeps them connected to the world.

WIRED TO SERVE

Connection is the key ingredient to service. By the way, we can only serve each other by relating; hence the term, relationships. We must connect to relate. We must relate to serve. And there must be a relationship in order for you to serve your gift effectively. We are spiritual beings who are wired spiritually and physically to connect with other people.

In terms of information, anyone who desires to have access to the web's resources must be connected or have some means of connectivity. This could be hardwired or done through a mobile or wireless device. Religion in this case can be viewed as the *hardwire connection,* where a medium (of rituals with good works attached) is required in order to have direct access to salvation.

Let's clarify one thing right now: *you can never do enough good to receive salvation or make it into heaven.* Stop trying to get into heaven. That is religion. Heaven is not just a place with some pearly gates you simply enter into by ringing a fancy bell on the big front gate and out comes a "god-like-figure" or angelic being, who beams you up through the clouds like Star Trek so you can live long and prosper.

Doing good deeds is not a requirement to salvation. However, they are a manifestation of the fruit of the Spirit working in your life. This is a direct result of having salvation by faith, through a divinely connected relationship with your Creator, the ultimate satellite and server through which all communication devices (like people) connect and share.

It is not religion, but a direct relationship to the vine, Jesus (*John 15:1*), that keeps you connected and provides the right nutrients to make you function and bear much fruit. God gets glory when you bear fruit, but fruitfulness requires growth and spiritual maturity.

MOBILITY AND CONNECTIVITY

"Growth and Maturity"

Mobility is just as important as connectivity. Think of the process this way: the hardwire connection permits a direct connection to the source, however, it is very limited and does not allow access unless you are physically connected to a confined space and location. But in order to grow you must be mobile, flexible and be willing to adjust. Mobility requires movement and growth comes with the increase of knowledge which is downloaded only to those who are unrestrictedly connected to the source. To put it plainly, you must be present to receive; thus, the religious hardwire connection restricts and lacks flexibility, creativity and spiritual advancement and growth.

For this reason, many churchgoers fail to grow. They become spiritually dormant, stagnant and over time simply fall off the religious bandwagon. Therefore, their connection to the source (server) is solely based on *"religiously"* doing just enough good works (which is a reflection of the length of their Ethernet cable) to receive connectivity. You may be connected, but without growth, renewal of mind and body, death is inevitable. To avoid this you must be willing to go beyond mere duty.

GO BEYOND DUTY

Doing just enough charitable good is identical to having just the right length of Ethernet cable to reach your (*god-source*) server. Otherwise, your connection is severed the moment you grow (mature) or move from your fixed location. To get "religious" updates and doctrinal downloads, just like any computer device, the individual must return to the medium (a church, priest or place of corporate worship and confess) and reconnect to access the life-sustaining resources to continue living.

Not only are you limited through *hardwire-religion*, you become powerless, trapped and unable to function to the best of your God-given ability. You become dormant and unable to grow; the end result is a life without fruit. You are therefore unfit to minister (serve) others who desperately need your area of giftedness and expertise to survive. You were not designed to be religiously stationary and immobile, but to go beyond rituals and routine to accomplish amazing feats for the glory of God. *"Verily, verily, I say unto you, He that believeth on me, the works that I do shall he do also; and greater works than these shall he do..."* (John 14:12a) Instead of you being the doctor, teacher and parent, you remain the patient, the student and the child, unable to transition from milk to meat.

Paul laments this stagnant condition, *"...By this time you ought to be teachers, you need someone to teach you the elementary truths of God's word all over again. You need milk, not solid food!"* (Hebrews 5:12) When there is no growth, your spiritual gifts and talents become obscure, hidden and masked.

Treasures are hidden because people are simply gathering and not connecting. The truth is, *believers don't go to church; for they, like the body, are members and parts of the whole organism, which assembles and connect in communities to make the entire body work more efficiently to fulfill the kingdom mandate...to do greater works than Jesus did.*

The real church, which is the body of Christ, does not attend congregational settings or sit in arranged pews just for emotional wellbeing and feel-good assemblies. Similar to the vital organs in the human body, the body of the kingdom assembles with a divine purpose to use their individual giftedness to build, serve, and to do a work that honors the Creator.

CONNECT TO ACCESS

Access to reliable connection is fundamental to living abundantly. This is only possible when a complete body has all its members properly functioning at their optimal best. Therefore, a great product is a direct result of having great components and the right building blocks. Additionally, a body without visual acuity lacks vision and is in darkness.

"The eye is the lamp of the body; so then if your eye is clear, your whole body will be full of light. But if your eye is bad, your whole body will be full of darkness. If then the light that is in you is darkness, how great is the darkness!" (Matt. 6:22-23) As a result, a body that lacks vision is incomplete and susceptible to malfunction. What I am saying to you is this; good members (of the body) who function will assemble to make the whole body good and function even better.

Therefore, a product, just like the body, is only as good and effective as the parts from which it is made. This means, the real purpose for coming together as members of the one body is to connect with other believers who have diverse gifts, talents and skillsets to make the whole body more efficient when all the parts connect to access the resources that each individual member brings.

For this reason, you must bring both your "A-GAME" and your best gift when you assemble. Mediocrity has no place in the kingdom of God and the kingdom community. Why? Because Organic Chemistry teaches us that a limiting reagent who's total chemical reactions are limited by the slowest agent will go at the speed of the slowest reactant. Quality determines output; likewise, the body becomes limited and weakened by doubt, doublemindedness, and discourse. This is why unity (being on one accord) improves strength, efficiency and provides the greatest support. There's strength in numbers and the ultimate goal of assembling is to become one.

You cannot access what you are not connected to. You cannot participate in any community if you simply say to yourself *"Oh, I just came to look."* You cannot get involved in your church or community if you just attend and never serve in that community. Access therefore is a result of having fundamental connectivity through the sharing of vital resources. If you are not connecting with people, you cannot access the abundant resources that are readily available to you through people.

WHERE HIDDEN TREASURES CONNECT

Figuratively speaking, the wealthiest place on earth could be the graveyard because of the abundance of unused gifts, untapped potential and incomplete dreams. I also believe however, that there is something even more profound than the graveyard; it is here and now, the present, the living. Ultimately, the wealthiest environment is not a place or a specific location; it is in the living, people who are alive. Why? because those who are alive still have a chance to change the future. The dead no longer participates in the flourishing of humanity and the building up of a community. *"It is not the dead who praise the LORD..."* (Psalm 15:17).

One might also argue that, *"If the dead nourishes the plants that provide the oxygen we breathe, don't they contribute to humanity?"* To a certain extent, yes, but the ability to serve other humans in a community cannot be done by the dead. You on the other hand, are not mulch for trees, you are alive and your life is a treasure to everyone who seeks and a lifeline to a dying world.

Just in case you have not already met, may I introduce you to the wealthiest beings in all of creation?—**YOU and the people you meet daily**! Your neighbor, your loved ones, the stranger on the street, even that old decrepit person struggling to make it across the street is wealthy. The problem is that the wealth is still trapped on the inside of many people and it may never be released until accessed by others. It is our past which affects our present, but the future is determined by the choices we make and the actions we take today. Not tomorrow but today! Connection creates access that causes divine revelations to be downloaded for your development, but growth and prosperity can only come through effective use of your downloads.

Here is a statement that may shock you: *Your abundance is not in heaven, it is inside each individual that makes up the body of Christ in a kingdom community.* The treasures are trapped in people. *God is great* but his greatness is also a part of you and your neighbors' DNA, their genetic makeup. This is why you must *love your neighbor as you love yourself* because in doing so, you simply love God and his extended greatness that is trapped inside all of us. One of the best things about a treasure is that it is always connected to wealth, and if you are connected to God, you are wealthier than you think. This is why, *"We have this treasure in (jars of clay) earthen vessels, so that the surpassing greatness of the power will be of God and not from ourselves"* (2 Corinthians 4:7).

THE KEY TO YOUR FUTURE
The Next Person You Meet

We are to esteem one another more highly than ourselves. The late Dr. Myles Munroe always said *"If you really knew who I was you'd take me to lunch."* What he meant is simply this: You never know who you are sitting, standing or walking next to until the fruit is revealed—and if everyone is *"fearfully and wonderfully made"* (Psalm 139:14), then everyone has supernatural greatness trapped on the inside of him or her and you will never know until you connect. *If you disregard people as nobodies, you may have simply cancelled your future.*

TREAT PEOPLE RIGHT
Treating people right and making them feel special is not a matter of religion nor does it make you religious; it's a way of life that makes living accessible and more enjoyable for everyone. Think of people as organ donors and you are the recipient who desperately needs a heart, kidney, or lung transplant to stay alive. The only problem is that you don't know it as yet and only time will tell. If in your daily interactions you have unknowingly mistreated your donor, your future could be looking very grim.

Let's use our imaginations for a minute and just think of what could happen if later on your death bed, and moments before you take your last breath, you looked over and their standing over you were the people you ridiculed and mistreated before you succumbed to your final resting place. You are now on the verge of joining the other dead who will no longer participate in improving the world. To your surprise, the very thing you needed to restore your health and maintain your well-being was right in front of you…and even better, they were willing and more than happy to be your donor…just think how your final moments would be. I think you get the picture. Sad, isn't it? Absolutely…sad!

Religion will tell you to do good deeds, but that is not *"gonna"* cut it if your deeds are not genuinely done from a place of purity and love. Unlike religion where work-centered salvation is your ticket to the afterlife, good works alone is never the central focus of the kingdom of God, love is.

The *Spirit* of love is a direct result of the function of the fruit of the *Spirit* operating in your life through optimal kingdom connectivity. Good deeds therefore, are not a requirement, they are however, results of the *Spirit* that manifests itself when members in the body of Christ support each other by accessing the abundant resources available through the giftedness and expertise that each joint supplies. The body is only as strong as the connective tissues that mend it together (*ACTOOO, Atoms, cells, tissues, organs, organ-systems, that make up the organism*) and you are one of them.

What you need is right next to you, the people you meet every day. Stop overloading the prayer line, asking God to send down a blessing for you; instead, you should be asking for divine clarity and direction to locate the abundant resources that is trapped in people (*earthen vessels*) and waiting for you to access them from one or a group of members in the body.

The heart does not need to look outside of the body to get nutrients to feed its muscle cells. It simply looks inside the body of which it is a member, becomes a pump and creates its own supply as it connects to the body's abundant resources.

One of the concepts of the anatomy of the kingdom is that everything you need is readily available to you and it is accessible through serving. **Giving is the new Receiving and serving is the new believing.** Serving others is to serve oneself. Loving others is to love oneself. If you really believe that, then you would do anything for your fellowman or woman with zero expectation. Serve from a place of love, withholding nothing.

To merely say that the heart is religiously *"doing a good deed"* to receive *"salvation"* in the form of returned blood to feed its pumping muscle cells is absurd. It receives because it gives; the heart gets its nourishment by serving other members in the same body. We call this a *symbiotically mutualistic interaction (SMI)*, a cooperative exchange. Notice, during a brisk walk your heartrate may slightly increase but a sprint will quickly raise your heartrate to its maximum output.

We know this in exercise physiology as [HRmax] where the heart increases its delivery to match the demand that the body puts on it. The heart therefore, can be physiologically referred to as a responder to any circumstance the body experiences. The quicker, harder and faster the heart pumps and serves, the quicker, harder and faster the heart receives blood as the body returns it back to the working muscle tissue of the heart. This means that the heart gives the body cells what they require to maintain life (for the whole body) as it receives bountifully from its pumping labor. We call this a *labor of love*.

Let's dig a little deeper. Shall we? Because the heart's main function is to serve the body as a pump in the circulatory system, it receives nutrients in return for serving. The same is true for us. You do not have to go to heaven to get a kidney transplant; unless God supernaturally creates one for you, whatever you need is here on earth. You just have to want it and then assemble and connect to have direct access. Like a diamond, sometimes you have to dig through the rough (see past the bad) to access the good in every man; so the luster will only be seen when you connect.

NOTES

Chapter 10. Kingdom Connectivity

1. Dewey, Caitlin. "Almost as Many People Use Facebook as Live in the Entire Country of China." Washingtonpost.com, 29 Oct. 2014. Web. (Accessed, 14 Nov. 2015).

PART- IV

EXCHANGING RELIGION FOR A LIFE OF FUNCTION AND PURPOSE
"Choice Is King"

CHAPTER 11

THE "R" WORD THAT RULES THE WORLD

"God expects his people to live victoriously and confidently."
~Dr. Lester Sumrall

The true purpose for coming together is to create lasting communities; otherwise, we just have social gatherings that are a futile recurring pass-time. With this in mind, we should always examine the purpose and the outcome of our religious assemblies. Religion, in the context of this book, is an *organized synthetic system of worldly controls based on beliefs and convictions established to institutionalize its participants.*

This same "*Religion*" is the "R" word that rules the world. However, as you will learn, it is also a repellant to the human spirit. Instead of bridging the gap to bring humanity closer to one united front, religion discriminates, it separates and dominates the human spirit and reduces it to mere duty-conscious hope. The foundation of religion is built on the notion that tomorrow things will change if only you follow a set of doctrines today; then somehow you will make it to heaven when you die. This conundrum of spiritualism has been the driving force of religion. From pre-historic to modern times, religion has played an enormous role in shaping the world and people's perception of God. It is a perpetual cycle that never changes; you simply wash, rinse and repeat.

The greatest tragedy about "R" is that lives are at stake, souls are hanging in the balance scale of eternal peril, while billions of dollars and other natural resources are squandered every day to propagate this travesty of the kingdom of God.

TRADITIONALIZED SPIRITUALITY

The traditionalizing of spirituality is a crippling force to the human spirit. It leads many to wander like indecisive skeptics who live on the fence of insecurity and have become spiritually confused. This confusion is the intended function of religion. As a result, millions lose hope because they have been searching for external proof to justify a form of god and have come up shorthanded. Why? Because they are misguided. But *"God is not the author of confusion, but of peace, as in all churches of the saints"* (1 Corinthians 14:33*).* However, if one can create a system that confuses you to a point of surrender, the battle for the soul is already won.

The greatest battle of spirituality goes beyond doctrines and religious labels; the real fight is fueled by questions in the warzone of the mind. Unanswered questions lead to doubt and prolonged doubts lead to fear.

ONE IN CHRIST-DIVIDED IN RELIGION

Why can't we just celebrate what makes us one, what makes us better and the traits that make us more similar than different? That is a great place to start, but more people continue to hide behind religion instead of facing the facts.

The fact is we are called to be ONE in Christ, one big family of God in the earth. But the reality is that there are more divisions and disharmonies among religious denominations than there are plaids to make a kilt. There is a global pandemic; the fundamental meaning of family is under unyielding attacks.

Dysfunctional educational systems are on the rise and there are more broken marriages and haphazard relationships than ever. This is happening as you read this book and it will not get better unless a massive shift in spiritual consciousness occurs.

Now, I completely understand that this will ruffle some of your religious feathers. But you miss the true meaning of living and the value of life when you put the practice before the practitioner and the practitioner before the Creator. In other words, it is not wise to put a religion or denomination before the human, and humanity before his creator, GOD. In the order of operation, (whether scientific or spiritual), God is supreme and everything is a result of Him. Not all are in God but everything came out of him, this includes you.

In essence, the practice of religion does not allow you to see people for who they truly are: *spirit beings full of potential, unique, and a gift to the kingdom community called the body of Christ.* Religion sees only the differences in humanity and classifies them based on tradition. God's Kingdom, however, embraces our likeness and recognizes our differences. It also highlights how each of us equally has a unique function in the body. Religion, sees us as different and persuades us not to work together. In fact, let us destroy each other; let us harass, mangle, hate and kill anyone who opposes our doctrine or way of **perceived holiness**—all in the name of a differentiated practice (religion) that penalizes humanity for being uniquely gifted and equally different. Hence, many have lost their way in search of faith and spirituality.

If you follow religion, you will miss people. But if you discover the kingdom of God, you'll truly see God abundantly in all of His glorious awe and splendid creation. I encourage you to go back and reread the section on community. It truly is an eye opener.

The kingdom of God is a fluid community that is alive. In God we move, we live and have our being. This is the kingdom in motion. It is alive in you and me. Like any anatomical structure of the human body you could be the heart, lung, kidney, brain or eyes; regardless of your structure, we are all part of this body collectively. And when we function and play our assigned roles, we create a harmonious mosaic work of art that brings joy to the Creator's heart. Every member is specially equipped to make the body live. From cells to tissues, organs and organ systems, to the living organism, the kingdom breathes life, whereas religion takes it away. Religion is not your answer to knowing GOD personally.

THE NEW DESIRE IS TRUTH

It is my belief that people truly want to have a working knowledge of God and to experience the reality of Him working in their lives. The new desire is no longer the afterlife; it is truth. But religion, in search of spirituality, has cast a veil over the eyes of people transforming them into spiritual zombies.

The mere mention of some religious denominations cause hearers to cringe because they have actually been trained to shun the restrictive beliefs of others. If we are reading the same Holy Bible and truly believe that Jesus is the son of God, the words of Paul in 1 Cor. 12:12-14 should cause us to see that religion is divisive. *"For as the body is one, and hath many members, and all the members of the body, being many, are one body; so also is Christ…in one Spirit were we all baptized into one body, whether Jews or Greeks, whether bond or free; and were all made to drink of one Spirit…the body is not one member, but many."*

My hope is that you do not settle for just a religion by conforming to denominational doctrines that defy the truth of the word of God. But that you discover God and function to the best of your ability with divine purpose.

There's more to life and much more to living when you understand who you are and the God who made you. But to experience this you must have a desire to want more; dig deeper, and seek to find truth. *Remember, information is plenty, knowledge is abundant but truth is rare.* Don't just settle. You owe it to yourself to have a working knowledge of who you are, the truth about your Creator and your purpose for living. As a product of the kingdom, your greatest pursuit is to discover what you were made to do.

I do not suggest you leave this to chance or the local preacher, hoping that it will happen by osmosis. You will always find when you seek. *"Ask, and it shall be given you; seek, and ye shall find; knock, and it shall be opened unto you: for every one that asketh receiveth; and he that seeketh findeth; and to him that knocketh it shall be opened." (Matthew 7:7-8 KJV)* You just have to start. Get busy living or life will pass you by.

RESEARCH ON RELIGION

My research about the role of religion and how people are affected by it over time was very insightful. Did you know that over eighty-five percent of the world's population is linked to some form of religion or type of practice, which emphasizes spiritual wellbeing? [1] Of those, less than 35% believe in one God. Early practitioners of religion believed religion was the way to connect the human spirit to the unknown.

Many drew paintings, carved out images in caves, built monuments like the Stonehenge and made temples and other artifacts to practice what they thought was the ultimate way to reach their god and experience enlightenment. Some had special rituals, dances, chants and music that were used to bring spiritual enlightenment.

Unlike other polytheistic and unaffiliated religions, Christianity is a monotheistic philosophy that is practiced by over two billion people worldwide. According to an April 2015 article by the *PEW Research Center*, (a nonpartisan fact tank) titled *"The Future of World Religions: Population Growth Projections, 2010-2050"* stated that Christians will remain the largest religious group for the next four decades.² PEW also projected that Islam, being the second largest religion, will see substantial growth due to geographic distribution and population growth trends.

PEW Research (Pewresearch.org), compared the changes among the various religious groups based on projected shifts in global population. In addition to population sizes, the number of people who practice a certain kind of religion is grossly impacted as people switch from one faith to another.³ It goes to show that even though there are thousands of world regions, people are still not content spiritually and will continue to flip-flop from faith to faith because they are desperately searching for truth.

THE PROJECTED FUTURE OF RELIGION

PEW projected that, with the exception of Buddhists, all of the major religious groups are expected to increase in number by 2050. Still, some will not keep pace with global population growth; as a result, many are expected to make up a smaller percentage of the world's population in 2050 that they did in 2010.

Approximately 32% of the world's population will be Christian and about 30% Muslim. That's an astounding 62% of the world controlled by two beliefs. The rest, which is about 38% are Buddhists, folk religion and unaffiliated practices.

So, what does this global shift look like numerically? Additionally, PEW stated that there are about 2.17 billion Christians in the world and that number is projected to increase by roughly .75 to about 2.95 billion by 2050. Likewise, there are approximately 1.6 billion Muslims and this number is also projected to increase to nearly 2.75 billion by 2050.

One of the main reasons for this massive shift in faith, I believe, is due to the induced fear that religion projects on participants. Fear of the unknown or the proverbial *"afterlife"* is one of the root causes, which motivates people to join a religion.

Consequently, their hope is that the practice of a religion will save them or provide a purgatory that will pacify their spiritual uncertainty in the meantime. But hope is not discovered in the practice of any religion, it is found in God, the Creator. Hope does not come by a religion; it is through a divine relationship with Christ. *(...Christ in you, the hope of glory."* (Colossians 1:27b)

I believe it was the Creator's intent for us to live the present life now, today, instead of some unknown tomorrow. I can only image what today would be like if we devoted the quality time to live the present life to its fullest, then the afterlife would take care of itself. It's like saying, I am alive now but I will wait until tomorrow to live. I have eyes now but I will wait for tomorrow to see. I have a brain but thinking is better off done tomorrow. God wants you and I to live now and to do all that he has placed in our hearts to accomplish in this lifetime.

A SHIFT TO PURPOSE AND FUNCTION

While traditions vary, for the most part, all religions have one thing in common, the quest to find some form of medium or conduit outside of humanity to gain spirituality and to answer life's most profound questions: "Why am I here?...To do what?...and how do I do it? Aside from traditional practices, many believe that religion has a place in society and plays a significant role. Many believe it provides hope, creates order and brings meaning to life.

On the other hand, it is my belief that the world needs more than hope, safety nets and rituals. People need awareness of their gifts so they can function and discover their purpose to fulfill their life assignment.

Therefore, the answers to life's daunting questions are not out there; they are in there (inside of you, where God put them), waiting for you to discover, develop and effectively use them to make God's kingdom your earthly reality that supersedes religion and nullifies any practice and thought of ever looking elsewhere to find Him.

EVERY DAY IS HOLY.
It is a gift to you and a blessing to your eyes
So long as it is visible

Any practice that separates you from God, (the creation from its Creator), or divides and discriminates against others because of insignificant doctrinal differences, such as the day of worship, or dietary choice, seeks to harm humanity more than help. The apostle Paul addressed this same issue of petty divisions within the church quite firmly throughout his writings. I especially want to highlight some verses from the book of Romans chapter 14:

> *"Who are you to judge someone else's servant? To their own master, servants stand or fall. And they will stand, for the Lord is able to make them stand."* Romans 14:4

Paul continues, in Romans 14: 6-10: *"Whoever regards one day as special does so to the Lord. Whoever eats meat does so to the Lord, for they give thanks to God; and whoever abstains does so to the Lord and gives thanks to God. For none of us lives for ourselves alone, and none of us dies for ourselves alone. If we live, we live for the Lord; and if we die, we die for the Lord. So, whether we live or die, we belong to the Lord. For this very reason, Christ died and returned to life so that he might be the Lord of both the dead and the living. You, then, why do you judge your brother or sister? Or why do you treat them with contempt? For we will all stand before God's judgment seat."*

I am reminded of the story of the Good Samaritan, who was not religious but had a deep connection and empathy for humanity. He saw no difference between the wounded man and himself and spared no expenses but did for a total stranger what he would want someone to do for him. The Good Samaritan is a profound example of the kingdom in motion and the power of community in action. The fact that Jesus highlighted such neighborly behavior in the story demonstrates its significance to kingdom living.

This concept of goodness in action is extremely relevant to every race and nationality, our community, society as a whole and the world at large. No religion can impart this wisdom to you; serving your neighbor is beyond a good deed, it is a function of your spirit that becomes visible when you bear fruit. Your gift is a spiritual seed that produces the fruit when you serve. This is the principle that Jesus emphasized throughout his teachings. This is not a religion, but a way of life for the kingdom of God in motion.

NOTES

Chapter 11. The "R" word that rules the world

1. Sumrall, Lester. *The Names of GOD.* New Kensington, PA: Whitaker House, 1982. (P 181).

2. Star, Fleur. *What Do You Believe?* London: DK, 2011. Print

3. "The Future of World Religions: Population Growth Projections, 2010-2050." *Pew Research Centers Religion Public Life Project RSS.* 2015. Web. 06 Oct. 2015.

*EXCHANGING RELIGION
FOR A LIFE OF FUNCTION AND PURPOSE*

Your gift is a spiritual seed that produces fruit when you serve. It will remain dormant until... You decide!

~Andrew E. Guy

Whether you choose to win or lose, or simply do nothing at all, in the end the choice has always been yours.

~Andrew E. Guy

CHAPTER 12

THE PATH TO TRUTH

Seekers Always Find

THE END OF SPIRITUALITY IS RELIGION. Although plausibly, there could be no end to spirituality, because we are spirit beings. However, since religion is not the answer, the only way to truly transform your life, function with purpose and be fulfilled, is to seek to know yourself, discover your area of giftedness (your function) and then get busy living it.

One of my favorite actors, Morgan Freeman, from the movie *Shawshank Redemption*, said it best: *"Get busy living or get busy dying..."* [1] As for me, I choose life, and you should too. In fact, God wants you to have more than just ordinary living. His desire for you is that you live victoriously and have life more abundantly; so much more abundantly that ***you will spend the rest of your waking days giving it away as a service to others for the betterment of humanity.***

After several years of research and observation I've seen the damage and spiritual dismantling of the human spirit and I can't see how this pleases God. Manmade infrastructures are collapsing, people are switching faith, and families are ruined because of the ideological picture that religion paints. Many atrocities are carried out in the name of religion; which in fact, creates even more obscurity for those who have no real knowledge of God. These include some who claim to be followers of Jesus Christ.

During my quest, I came across a book by Jocelyn R. Zichterman. In brief, she tells a horrifying story of how she *"Fired God"* as result of her abusive encounter with her preacher-father, an influential member of a Christian denomination. She described the ruthlessness and the abuse she underwent that left her faithless, void of hope and full of fear. *"I wondered if there was a God,"*[2] she said.

Reading this book certainly ruffled my spiritual feathers and since then, left me grossly concerned about the state of spiritualism cloaked by religious indoctrination. A father who was supposed to love and cherish his little girl became a terrorizing force in her life, all because he thought he was doing the work of God under the influence of an indoctrination, which hailed him to be the authoritative figure who dealt justice.

Jocelyn is not alone. No, Jocelyn, you are not alone in this religious upheaval and dismantling of the human spirit. There are others; in fact, there are millions more out there hiding behind the curtains of a religion and denominational sect. It is my hope that they find the freedom to step out from the crowd and be the individuals who experience the *Kingdom* of God in such a personal way that their lives are transformed.

It is my belief that people are no longer searching for temporary quick fixes, or Band-Aids of religious labels to cover up their spiritual void. They desperately want truth. With great hope, seekers are venturing into church buildings by the droves to hear the local preacher give a soul-convicting sermon.

It is imperative, however that seekers understand that their search for God should not be based on psychological pressures created by societal practices, but an individual quest for knowing and developing a personal relationship with the Creator.

Therefore, truly seeking God means to relinquish what you *think* you know about him (because that is only a limited version) and create a presence that invites his Spirit to take up residence in you when you seek him with all your heart. Do not do this to please others; do it to help yourself. After all, having done so, you will be able help someone else.

You will need more than "just" faith to seek God; you will also need to have a working knowledge of what he said about you and who he says he is. God of all creation. It is also important to note that the size of the church building you attend or the number of people in attendance is no indication of your level of spirituality or holiness.

THE CAPACITY FOR GROWTH

There is a greater capacity for personal growth and spiritual development than previous times. Today more than ever, telecommunication outlets are flooded with broadcasting sermons. At the same rate, churches are bursting at the seams with soul-searchers. This thirst for spiritual growth and self-improvement has become a multi-million dollar empire to a few elite orators. As the demand increases, no longer does the average *church-building* with towering steeples suffice for "Sunday-Worship." Giant stadiums are now the in-thing; massive buildings with capacities in the thousands and the demand for more is still growing. *"The very largest U.S. churches draw more than 30,000 to worship each weekend,"* [1] the Hartford Institute For Religion Research reported in 2015.

The result of this enlarged appetite for spiritual gathering has now been coined into a phrase called *"Mega-Church."* But could the size of a congregation pose a threat to people's faith and spiritual development? Without the right leadership, I imagine it could. Larger groups require additional staff support that is qualified to lead and nurture the sheep.

It could also be argued that with the rise in population growth, having a bigger church is better. No pun intended, but if it's okay for sporting events, it is justifiable to have large buildings for mega religious gatherings. Right? Speaking of which, did you know that one of the world's largest sporting venue, having a seating capacity of approximately 400,000 is the *Indianapolis Motor Speedway?* [2] That's almost a half-a-million people in one place! Moreover, Salt Lake Stadium in Kolkata, India is the largest multi-functional soccer stadium in the world according to www.sportskeeda.com.

On the contrary, this whole notion of big versus small buildings results in finger pointing. Small churches condemn mega-churches for their building sizes, but small churches should also examine their level of influence in their communities. In retrospect of community spirit, there is a major question that could be asked of smaller churches. What are you doing to address the disparities of the people in your neighborhood?

Could it be that small churches have become so comfortable at *"having church"* that they fail to reach out to the "outsiders" and as a result end up on the short end of the attendance scale? What do you think? Are smaller churches doing their due diligence to adapt to the changing times to bring more people into the fold and grow their congregation?

Alternatively, are mega-churches more concerned with attendance size as opposed to the spiritual growth and development of their members? Then again, does it even matter if a church body is MEGA or Meager?

One might also argue that society and the unchurched world should have no qualms over religious organizations having such large buildings for corporate gatherings, so long as there's a need for it; plus, if so many people who are lost and confused suddenly discover the urgency to prepare for the afterlife, where will we house them?

Consequently, one of the primary concerns should be whether those who are supposed to be served by the church (big or small) are being served. Similarly, what standards (if any) are in place to measure the spiritual growth of a congregation, their commitment to service and community interaction? How does the size of a church affect this aspect of spirituality?

REACHING THE MASSES

Size does play a significant role in quality of service. With larger crowd comes bigger responsibility. What are the processes being utilized to reach the masses? According to the *Megachurches 2015 Summary Report*, a study done by Scott Thumma, Ph.D. and Warren Bird, Ph.D. of the Hartford Institute For Religion Research, *"Very large churches face many of the same challenges as congregations of other sizes. Additionally, their large size makes aspects of their religious work that much more difficult, such as creating commitment, community, and member engagement."* [3]

To address the concerns of having a larger than normal following, most mega-churches are now implementing cell groups or what's known as small groups to accommodate the increase in membership size. Within these cell groups, newcomers especially have the opportunity to receive the necessary training to aid their development.

One example of cell groups in action is *The Yoido Full Gospel Church* in Seoul, South Korea, led by Pastor D. Yonggi Cho. It is the largest church in the world, and home to more than a half-a-million members. Dr. D. Yonggi Cho (author of *Successful Home Cell Groups*) accredits the use of small groups for the effective growth and sustaining of his supersized congregation.

This approach could also be effective in large and small congregations, plus, small groups provide additional opportunities for members to become more acquainted in their communities. Another benefit to smaller size groupings can be seen in breakout sessions, which are utilized to emphasize vital information that may have been missed during the general assembly.

There are obviously efforts being made to shepherd the mega-church. Still, several questions arise: Is the church positively affecting its community and surroundings? Are people finding what they came for? And how do they even know whether or not they've made the connection to spirituality? Who should we hold accountable, the preacher, the leaders, the first lady or the usher? Who...?

MEGA-ACCOUNTABILITY

One might also contend that, even though the corporate church plays a role in the development of its people, it is not responsible for your spirituality or soul. As a collective body you are your *brother's keeper*, but the power of choice makes you a free agent and personally liable for your own growth.

You are the only one that is responsible for your actions; even preachers must work out their own salvation. So, there is a mega responsibility for each person to be personally accountable. **When you begin to take responsibility for your personal growth, you will discover the confidence to find truth.**

Timothy reminds us about the importance of self-accountability in pursuit of truth: *"Study to shew thyself approved unto God, a workman that needeth not to be ashamed, rightly dividing the word of truth"* (2 Timothy 2:15 KJV). This is why it is vital that you know God for yourself. Not through the lens of a religion, but through developing a personal relationship with him.

No one said it would be easy, but every believer knows that the fight of faith is life's greatest challenge. It is no walk in the park and you must be willing to defend it. *"Fight the good fight of the faith. Take hold of the eternal life to which you were called when you made your good confession in the presence of many witnesses"* (1 Timothy 6:12).

Spiritual wellness is a full contact sport and a battle for the soul you must win.

SPIRITUAL ENDURANCE TO OVERCOME

Most preachers do their best to help their congregations make some spiritual connection between what is preached, what is perceived, and what is received. In essence, what is preached is the method used by the preacher to inform the listener; what is perceived is what the listener believes the lesson is about; and what is received is the final takeaway message that the listener retains.

Spiritual endurance is a decision every individual must make. Choice is king, and at the end of the day, everything is entirely up to you. Therefore, s*piritual wellness is a full contact sport and a battle for the soul that you must win.*

This is one fight you cannot afford to lose. But are you in shape to contend, and do you possess the spiritual endurance to overcome? You will need all the encouragement you can get because *Heaven Ain't No Walk In The Park!* And there's no room for sideline spectators here.

Being a hearer is only a fraction of the battle. You must become an active doer. Everything is riding on this: it is your soul, your spirit, your body, your God, and your search for fulfillment and living with divine purpose.

I love the way James reinforces this concept of true self-identification coupled with community and the kingdom in motion. *"For if any be a hearer of the word, and not a doer, he is like unto a man beholding his natural face in a glass...and straightway forgetteth what manner of man he was...Pure religion and undefiled before God and the Father is this, to visit the fatherless and widows....and to keep himself unspotted from the world"* (James 1:23-27 KJV).

This is why it is paramount that you know yourself, understand that you *were made to show off the Creator's glory* and become knowledgeable about God instead of settling for the dogma and ritualistic lifestyles offered to you on a *religious platter*. You must have a peculiar spiritual diet that is geared toward understanding your function and the ability to do it with all your might. Discover your purpose and get busy doing your life assignment now.

NOTES

Chapter 12. The Path To Truth

1. *The Shawshank Redemption*. Dir. Frank Darabont. By Frank Darabont. Perf. Tim Robbins, Morgan Freeman, Bob Gunton, and James Whitmore. Columbia Pictures, 1994. Film. Web.

2. Zichterman, Jocelyn. *I Fired God: My Life Inside--and Escape From--the Secret* World of the Independent Fundamental Baptist Cult. New York: St. Martin's Press, 2013.(p 2-15)

3. Thumma, Scott, Ph.D, and Warren Bird, Ph.D. "2015 Summary Research Report of Recent Shifts in America's Largest Protestant Churches." *2015 Summary Research Report of Recent Shifts in America's Largest Protestant Churches*. Hartford Institute for Religion Research, Hartford Seminary, 2 Dec. 2015. (06 Jan. 2016)

4. Cho, Yong-gi, and Harold Hostetler. *Successful Home Cell Groups*. Plainfield, NJ: Logos International, 1981. Print.

CHAPTER 13

IN PURSUIT OF AUTHENTICITY
Spiritual Truth

Knowing yourself brings you that much closer to your gift, but understanding your gift reveals your Creator.
~*Andrew E. Guy*

You are going to have to make a decision to live for religion or live a life of function and purpose. Remember, one of the roles of religion is to keep you confused and interested long enough for you to lose sight of the *real* God. Imposters are everywhere and one of the never-ending battles of life is not about survival of the fittest, but the fight for what is *REAL*. I call it *Spiritual Authenticity*!

Do you remember the story of Elijah and the prophets of *Baal*? It was an event that highlighted the authentic power of God in the lives of those who trusted in him. Allow me to paraphrase. (Brace yourself because this is funny). I'm not sure what the weather was like, but it was a showdown on Mount Carmel, I kid you not! This was one of the biggest matches of all times. Bigger than Wrestle Mania, The World Olympics and the Pan-Am Games put together. This was *LUGE*!

The only thing that was missing from that faceoff was the world renowned Boxing ring announcer, Michael Buffer, to add his oratory intro and finishing touches. However, if Buffer were present, I imagined it would sound something like this: (the bell rings) *Ding! Ding! Ding...!* "*Let's Get Ready to Rumble!* (The crowed goes wild) *And in this corner....wearing glory and honor, the omnipotent one, mighty in power and awe, the real God of Abraham and Isaac! Jehovah Nissi! Yahweh! The El Shaddai!"* (And the true believers went wild with cheers followed by a slight pause as Buffer continued) *"And in that corner..."*

At this time, Buffer, became slightly confused and turns to the contender and said: *("Pardon me, sir. The first one I know but, who are you? What's your name?* (There was a long pause....then Buffer replied) *Oh, I see...Bail...Bhall...ball...? Hmm, in-ter-es-ting god-name...Okay, I've got it now. It's, d-evil one, the...devil!")* "*And There you have it, folks.*" *Ding! Ding...!* The bell rings and then, "*Fight!*" said Buffer. *LOLer! (laugh-out-louder)*. Now there's a spiritual funny break for you.

But seriously, as it were in the days of Elijah, the people watched and wondered with great anticipation. Who's god would bring down the fire? The *"man-you-fractured"* (broken-man-made) god—or the *real Jehovah-Elyon,* the God of Abraham, Isaac and Jacob, the maker of both the wood, the fire and the man who made the altar.

The prophets of *Baal* tried everything (sang songs, danced, cried, pleaded and even cut themselves) but nothing worked. No fire, no power, no heat—they were all deadbeat.

Then Elijah told them to *"Stock up the wood and the sacrifice and pour the water; more please! A lot more,"* he insisted. (See 1 Kings 18). Then he called on the *real Jehovah God* of all god(s), the King of kings and Lord of lords and fire came down from the heavens and licked up everything, *DRY!* Wow! Fascinating, I thought. But just in case you didn't find this rendition rather amusing, a more serious version can be found in 1kings 18: 25-39.

All in all, there's a vast abundance of power available to each of us, and the goal here is to demonstrate that God wants to show off his glory in the lives of his people in the earth. Wallace D. Wattles once said that:

> *"God...is trying to live and do and enjoy things through humanity. He is saying "I want hands to build wonderful structures, to play divine harmonies, to paint glorious pictures; I want feet to run my errands, eyes to see my beauties, tongues to tell mighty truths and to sing marvelous songs..."* [1]

God wants to express his greatness through us, but those who follow man-made establishments will discover that all of their efforts are futile.

THE FAITH CHALLENGE

You may not be aware of this but every waking day of your life is a *showdown for your faith in the kingdom*. And who said it was going to be easy? Jesus is our example that, ***your faith is no walk in the park.*** Your faith will cost you. And you will pay one way or another. You just have to discard man-you-fractured religion and embrace God. Even if it were a bed of roses, you would have to appreciate that in the midst of great beauty (roses) there are still thorns.

THE FAITH WALK

Visible faith is belief in action. It produces something. Therefore, you must decide to take your stand as a visible part of the body in the kingdom. Visible faith is not just talk; it's about the walk. ***An invisible believer is similar to an absent organ and purpose without a function.*** There is no hiding behind the pretenses of religion. People and the world at large will come to know God when you function in the body. It turns out that being alive is not something you imagine—it is real.

Medical science tells us that a body is alive because your vital signs are a reflection that you are a living being. You have a heart rate, blood pressure, a pulse and a body temperature. These are signs of a living entity, all of which are absent in the dead. The same is true about faith. Like a muscle, faith must be exercised in order for it to grow and develop. Your faith will become the muscles which create the movements that propel you into your destiny.

Visible faith believes; it is alive and active. In fact, breathing is one of the greatest acts of faith, it is invisible to the naked eye but you breathe oxygen because you believe it will keep you alive. If you are not convinced that breathing is an act of faith, then deny yourself of oxygen. And if you really want to push the envelope, then tell yourself, *I see no God therefore I choose not to believe; I see no oxygen therefore I choose not to breathe.*

THE TREASURE WITHIN

People are much more powerful than they think, and far more intelligent than the concocted religions they choose to serve. God puts his treasure inside of us and it is our purpose to discover, develop and use to the glory of God.

Think about it. Why would you serve the fabricated practice of religion when "*it*" is less powerful than you are? Can "*it*" give you life? "*It*" cannot feed you, make you grow or strengthen you. Yet in a desperate search for purpose and meaning, a large majority has subserviently subscribed to the deceit of religion. And until we learn why we were created, *life is void of purpose and living becomes a costly experiment called effort.* You see, the urge to know God is not a reflection of the need for religion; rather, it is a built-in mechanism of the spirit to find its maker, to connect with its source. Until the source is found, wandering is inevitable.

The creator or "Source" of your spirit is *Jehovah* God. He is neither male nor female. He is a genderless Spirit who is often referred to as "*HE*" because he is the father of all things. Father means, creator, the progenitor and the giver of life. You and I are created in his likeness to reveal his glory in the earth. *"But we know that there is only one God, the Father, who created everything, and we live for him"* (1 Corinthians 8:6a NLT). He placed a gift inside of you that should be used to transform the world. Your goal in life is to discover, use and develop it. So where do you look for it?

Your greatest search is not out-there and it is definitely not in religion; it is *in-there* (inside of you). The religious map is a phantom guide that leads to nowhere. You want to know the worst part? There's no treasure at the end of its dogmatic, duty-focused rainbow. Unlike religion, you are the treasure in an earthen suit called a body, a replica of the kingdom of God, designed to create the culture of his kingdom on earth.

SEARCH NO MORE

The religious search for God has been a misguided quest that has uncovered *"manufactured"* god(s) instead of the *real* God who created all things. Religion is a manipulating orchestration that creates division between humanity and separates people from the *true* God.

It is vital that you understand both the purpose and the role of religion in society so that your living will not be in vain. There is only one God. Those who believe know him to be Abba Father, the one true Source and Giver of life, Founder, Creator, Author and Finisher of all.

Do not be confused by the many doctrines of religion that only serve as temporary bandages, which will not stick; they cover only the wounds of fear and confusion but do not address the cause of injury: ignorance. Consequently, you will find that many people continue to switch faith because they are hoping something will change for them in the process. But only truth is the solution.

If you are searching for God, please stop searching because He is not lost. ***You will run into God if you go way back before time began, and you will run into God if you escape into the future long after time ceases to exist.*** Before anything, there was God and after everything, there will always be God. The Creator exists in all creation, but the Spirit of God manifest himself in the life of the believer. We increase our awareness of God when we too acknowledge His presence and believe that He's a part of us. It is He who gives humanity the power to become the masterpiece that extends his will for us to make the kingdom in motion a *real* experience.

DISCOVER THE REAL CHURCH

The real church is not a location, but a limitless, borderless, "building-less" multicultural, diverse community; a collection of spirit-beings, who function like organs in the human body to fulfill a specific purpose to reveal the mind of the creator and make God's kingdom a reality.

As we have previously mentioned, in the context of this book, religion, is an "organized synthetic system of worldly controls based on beliefs and convictions established to institutionalize its participants." The Oxford English Dictionary defines religion as *"The recognition of superhuman controlling power of a personal god, entitled to obedience."* [2]

Unlike religion, the Kingdom of God is the system of Government that represents heaven. It is a function that is purposed to establish the presence of God in the earth. The practice of religion is counterproductive to kingdom function because instead of uniting the masses, it repels and dominates the human spirit.

Christianity is not defined as a religion, it is a philosophy. However, formations of Christian organizations called denominations and churches have religious elements because they are established on rules and regulations that are equally counter to kingdom function. Because religion has failed to bring humanity together, a Real church must emerge that has both the power and presence of oneness.

NOTES

Chapter 13: In Pursuit of Authenticity

1. Wattles, W. D. *The Science of Getting Rich:* Blacksburn, VA: Thrifty, 2009. (P. 22)

2. "Oxford English Dictionary defines religion:" http://www.oxforddictionaries.com/

CHAPTER 14

DYNAMIC PARTICIPANTS

"I want to know the mind of God in a mathematical equation... E=MC²"
~Albert Einstein

Have you ever wondered why *Facebook*, *LinkedIn*, *Twitter*, and *YouTube*, are the social media giants of the 21st century? Simple, they create communities that bring people together.

The real purpose of church is not just for you to show up with your fancy clothes or to see what others are sporting, but to be present. Social media is an example of what the "*Real Church*" should be; a place where people do more than just show up, they are present. *Contribution* is a sign of being engaged and actively present. When you are fully involved, it is a result of being mentally and spiritually present. Have you ever gotten hungry while you sat through a long church service and your mind left but your body was there? You can be there, without being there. Anyone can do that. The act of being present changes everything.

Anyone can *"show up."* But, being present is an act of service to your community. The tissues and surrounding community of the circulatory system benefit and receive nutrients because the heart did not just *show up*, it is present. Your five senses (plus those undiscovered) function and respond to stimulus because your brain did not just *show up*, it is present. The taste buds of the guests at your dinner banquet are well satisfied because the chef did more than just *show up*, he was present.

God is always present, but he becomes active when you are present. God is actively present in those who do more than just show up. You are the conduit that he works through to will and to do his good pleasure in the earth (see Philippians 2:13). It is part of God's function, to work in you, with you, through you, for his glory and for you to experience the joy of being an actively present participant.

This is what it means to receive strength from experiencing the joy of the Lord. It is impossible to be weak and be joyful at the same time. You have to be actively present to experience the joy of the Lord to receive your strength. It is the gift of God. The church (not a building, but a community) is the body through which he operates.

THE CHURCH THAT FUNCTIONS

As noted in the previous chapter, the *real* church is neither a building nor a component of some religious sect. The church that functions is active and dynamic. ***It is a living body of people with specialized gifts who serve each other.*** It is organic and sensitive to change; it is responsive. The real church is people. On the other hand, there are denominational organizations that operate as religious entities that define themselves as a church. But these are clearly not the *real* church. These are man-you-fractured organizations. They are religiously driven and their main focus is solely on the practice of a doctrine and not the well-being of the people who make up the community.

Today most denominational churches are losing members and will stand to lose millions more because they are not responsive to the concept of people-first. They are a rigid religion. Technologically speaking, did you know that *"responsivity"* (ability to adapt) is one of the highest standards by which search engine giants such as *Google* rank service and information?

Unlike the body, which adapts to climatic changes, viral attacks and adjusts to maintain life, many churches remain religiously rigid in their approach to meeting the needs of their community. Again, religion shows its evil head by saying, **"We are different from those people, so we don't mingle with them because we are unequally yoked."** Many religious church members have this perspective of being *"better-than"* others, and so, they become limited in their ability to function and serve in their communities.

THE CHURCH AND "STATE"

The *real church* gets involved in every area of living: *trade and commerce, politics, education, science and technology, health and wellness, personal and spiritual development, community planning and development, and actively participates in environmental issues that threaten humanity.* Why, you ask? Because Involvement is paramount in every area of living, including the above, is human orchestrated. There's no separation between the *real church* and state because they both impact each other.

The state is where we live but the church is who we are and how we function. The state can also be seen as the condition of a people, but the *real church* (an interconnected community) transforms people. Every piece of the puzzle that makes this planet livable is interconnected and vital to our well-being and survival. We are one body with many gifts and specific functions, but there is one God who made us for one purpose.

DRIVEN BY RESULTS

People are more driven by a function that produces results than being controlled by a practice. The "church" also known as, the body of Christ, is people-focused but *gift-specific*. Meaning, the world may value you as a human, but it is not you they want; it is the gift they are after. The gift is considered more valuable than the carrier of the gift. It is not the wrapper, but what's inside the package that is most valued. The sad reality is that most people may not be interested in you as a person, but they will consume your gift.

The same is true that the majority of people who practice religion could care less about the practice. It is God they are after and not the label of Christianity or some other religion. The disappointment arises when people get lost in the practice and miss God. Thirsty marathon runners could care less about the bottle that carries the water; they are after a thirst-quencher, the water trapped inside the bottle. Drivers of a Ford vehicle want a reliable vehicle that is consistent with their daily lifestyles. They are not concerned about Henry Ford or how many times he had to revisit his blueprints before creating the first Ford motor vehicle.

When the members of the church are present and the "body" functions, the world sees God. At the end of the day, true believers are least concerned about labels and prestigious titles; they really care more about function and results. The Good Samaritan (see Luke 10:25-37) is not remembered for his name, religious status or the amount of money he paid at the *Inn* to cover the expenses of the battered stranger he assisted; however, he is forever preserved in the minds of millions because of what he did, his function and the result of his service to the stranger.

DEVELOP PEOPLE BUT BUILD RELATIONSHIPS

A great majority of today's churches are clueless about their members. Even worse, communities are becoming more disenfranchised with their local church bodies because they are not being engaged socially and developmentally. Over the years, I have spoken with countless community members, professionals and working class alike, who no longer see the church as a viable entity for spiritual growth.

From my discussions, many seem to feel that religion is bent more towards conversion than building people and growing relationships. Many have taken a step forward to joining a church, but after becoming members, the routine of just *"churching-it"* begins and stagnation sets in. Some have even said, *"Yes, as an organization, the church wants you to join and they are excited at first, but after a couple of visits you become a regular church-goer."* No growth, no development, just *"churching-it,"* and hoping for a miracle.

I believe one of the primary reasons why there is such a massive disconnect between church leaders, members and the community is simply a lack of sincere concern for the needs of the stake-holders. The common agenda of most religions is driven by conversions, the number of souls saved. But what's missing is the relational piece of the puzzle that meets a greater need to develop the human beyond rituals and routine practices. Someone needs to begin the conversation to bridge the gap and engage our community.

So how do we start the conversation? A simple chat such as *"Hey, how are you? Are you new in the area or have you been here for some time now? Nice to meet you. My name is (fill in the blank) and I am from church/organization (a); we are reaching out to our community to (fill in the blank). What do you do for a living? If we can be of any assistance please let us know. Also, here are some activities that we do to engage our community. Learn more about us at (www. blah, blah blah...) or simply give us a call at...(provide a phone number) and you are done.*

You have just taken a huge step to engage your community by starting the conversation. It may look simple, but this first step is vital if you wish to connect with people. Not everyone needs a sermon, some just want to connect and feel connected. You could be amazed what a simple act like this can do.

Your goal is not to convert the masses, but to be the example. Conversion is the work of the Holy Spirit, not yours. Jesus did not set out to convert the masses. He simply met their needs (I want to see, said the *"blind"* man; I want to walk said the *"lame"* man...all these are needs) and by his actions (he healed the sick, fed the hunger, raised the dead, and inspired the poor) many believed. It is not the amount of scriptures you quote, but the lives that were transformed by your actions.

This could be one of the hundreds of ways you can engage someone in your community. Genuine communication should not be focused on converting the masses but meeting a need. There needs to be an authentic initiation of conversations between leaders of the church, its members and those of the community that is not based on joining a local church body, but create a supportive community-centered network that impacts the entire human being.

ASSIGNING GIFTS TO FUNCTION

Specialists with a purpose

Today there are millions of people attending church buildings. Many are inactive because no one really knows their function. On other hand, there are a few who actively serve, but in many cases, it is unfortunate that most of them are wrongfully assigned. They are busy doing the wrong things for the right reasons and so they are ineffective. Can you imagine if the heart were to do the job of the eye and the leg the function of the brain? **Talk about a bumpy sight for seeing and a kick in the head for thinking!**

"Now if the foot should say, "Because I am not a hand, I do not belong to the body," it would not for that reason stop being part of the body" (1 Corinthians 12:15). We are all *specialists* with *specific functions*. Therefore *"There are different kinds of spiritual gifts, but the same Spirit is the source of them all"* (1 Corinthians 12:4).

The *real church* in action should first become more aware of the fact everyone is gifted differently; as result be more consistent in matters of accountable. Leaders of the church should have an in-depth knowledge of who makes up the body: hands, eyes, feet, ears, and so on. An efficient church knows who is on their team and what gifts they have available for the body. A lack of this knowledge leads to stagnation and misuse of resources and gifts.

Pastors must become more in-tuned as leaders. The church is full of specialists without assigned roles. The *GP*, *general pastor*, was never capable of feeding the body (the sheep) and providing all the spiritual nutrition it needs. One-man/woman sermons do not meet the needs of every believer. The same is true that one size does not fit all.

This is why it is pertinent for GP's to have specialists come in to assist them in feeding the members (body) with the nutrients that keep them fit to run the race of life. There is a real life that exists outside the church walls and members must be prepared to live it effectively.

THE EFFECTIVE CHURCH

Today pastors serve as jacks-of-all-trades with few or no specialists to assist them. This type of leadership is ineffective and detrimental to the body of Christ as a whole. It leads to burnout and death.

Even Moses, the revolutionary leader of the Israelites, experienced this firsthand. I encourage you to read Exodus 18:13-27. It tells of the wise counsel Moses received from his father-in-law, Jethro, when the latter observed him sitting to judge all the people in the wilderness. *"What you are doing is not good,"* Jethro, warned. Then he proceeded to give young Moses what I consider to be the greatest advice a leader could ever get.

Leadership has little to do with leading people; it is, however, about establishing principles and living by examples for others to follow. To be an effective leader, you must assess the congregation to find out what gifts you have present among the members. Next, assign a committee to oversee ongoing training and development. This means, selecting qualified members to function based on their gifts to serve, edify, and build up the body. In order for the kingdom to be effective, leaders must know and understand the potential they possess.

If the mechanic has no idea he has a screwdriver in his tool kit, he will settle for a hammer to do the job of a screwdriver. Likewise, if the baker has no idea she has a measuring device, she will settle for a *dash of this or a pinch of that*. In the end, taste is comprised and too much of the wrong ingredient will always cause the bread to have an undesirable taste. The captain or leader should always know the strengths and weaknesses of his team the same way a general knows his army.

THE CURE FOR THE INEFFECTIVE CHURCH is to accurately assess available gifts, and assign specialized functions. Most churches have what's called a membership class, a way of *getting-to-know*, and informing the inductees of the ins and outs of the assembly they are about to join. This approach has its benefits and does provide for collecting basic information, but it is limited.

Plus, no good heart surgeon (cardiologist) simply jams an unchecked, used heart into the chest cavity of a patient without carefully assessing its condition before even starting the surgical procedure. Of course not. The highly qualified, board certified heart surgeon meticulously assesses the quality of the organ before transplanting it into the new patient's body. That way, the patient's body is efficiently served with richly pumped oxygenated blood by the newly transplanted heart.

JETHRO'S APPROACH

I truly believe that there's always room for improvement that leads to greater efficiency. Instead of just a membership form, new members should be required to submit a personal assessment in the form a resume, which consists of a list of their skills, values, goals and dreams and top five attributes. This information should then be used as a guide to assist the church body to effectively assign new members based on the needs of the church. I call this (*JAMLA*) the **Jethro-Anatomical Moses Leadership Approach.**

Too many people are simply going to church without knowing the real reason for attending. It's like saying the heart is in the chest cavity and doesn't know why, or the brain is inside of the skull but has no idea what thinking is; neither does it know how to send nerve impulses to other areas of the body to promote movement. Even better, you live in a house but have no idea which key unlocks your front door or how to work your microwave—clueless! Does that make any sense?

On the other hand, the *real church body* when fully assembled is self-sufficient, well-equipped and lacking nothing. Since this book is about the anatomy of the kingdom and how each interconnected part works together as a "whole-community," I believe it is fair to say that if the church, like the human body, was well equipped and assembled, then there should be little need for external interference. Moreover, the bank should not own the church building, the members should.

Everything that the body needs to maintain life is supplied and available: (*ACTOOO*: *Atoms, Cells, Tissue, Organs, Organ-*

System, Organism) and so it should be with the *real church*. This includes every profession and sector that deals with the community at large.

So, what am I saying here? **The real church is not a building, it's a people.** And anything that affects people should be a concern of the *real church*. If *today's church* ignores the real issues affecting its members then they (the members) will feel ill-supported and stranded; this leads to frustration and dismantling of the body, rendering it disease prone.

The frustration that most *churchgoers* of *the* man-you fractured organizations face is they believe that they are immune to struggles because they are religious. Quite frankly, the opposite is true. If you are alive and are human, you will have struggles but the good news is that (like working muscles in your body) you have help because "every joint" supplies what (you) the body needs, and your struggles build you up to make you stronger because it forces you to work together as one united body. Struggles are part of life and no one is exempt.

When the body undergoes strenuous activities such as when exercising, it recruits additional support from neighboring muscles to help facilitate movement and maintain function. The result is a stronger body with optimized coordination and improved capabilities. Faith does not excuse us from adversities they come to make us stronger.

A CORE FUNCTION THAT SERVES

Unlike the man-you fractured organizations with a haphazardous approach to "finding God", the *real church* has a core function that serves people in the form of a body called a community. The *Real church* is an effective body in action that utilizes the gifts, function and roles of its members.

The *real church* in action is a hospital to the sick, a place of restoration for the broken, a lifejacket to the novice swimmer, a map for the misguided and confused, and an environment conducive to the overall growth of humanity, not only the spiritual aspect. The kingdom in motion is the *anatomy and function* (physiology) of the *real church at work*. It is the body of Christ in action that creates an atmosphere and a culture that makes God visible in the earth. This function requires participation…you cannot just *show up*. You must be *present* for this to happen.

HAVING THE RIGHT "*AIM*"

The *real church* knows who is on the team and what gifts are available at all times and how to effectively delegate their administration. Leaders of the *real church* have an *Active Inventory Mindset* (*AIM*) of all its members, their gift, function and roles. This is similar to the body, where there are trillions of individual cells, and each has a specific function, and the body knows precisely where everyone is and how to access each function when necessary.

The body knows where to find the heart when it requires an increase of blood flow to support the working peripherals, lower and upper extremities. The body knows which muscle to activate when it needs to move in *fight or flight mode*, and what hormones to release to produce a certain behavior.

Just like the *real church*, organs of the body have specialized functions: the heart has a specific function, so does the brain, bladder, liver, kidney, spleen and stomach. Many of these individual organs aggregate (come together or team up) to form communities, which are also called interdependent body systems. For example, the heart serves in the community of the circulatory system; while the lung serves in the community of the respiratory system; in the same way that gastric juices serve in the community of the digestive system and the brain serves as CEO of the nervous system that relays information to other communities in the *"one"* body.

Does your *"church"* know your gift? Are they aware of your abilities? And are they being used to improve the people, who are the *real church* body? If you feel that you are not serving, or being served by your local church, you owe it to yourself to find out why. Moving to another church may not be the solution. You should definitely speak with your leaders to see what can be done about assessing and developing your gifts for service. When it comes to being part of the body and a member of any community, always remember this, *real* church has the right *"aim"* and so should you.

THE BIG PICTURE

No one lives for him or herself alone, but each of us is a thread in the fabric of life that makes living worth pursuing and life worth cherishing. Community begins when you put people first. Each person is an embodiment of the sum total of what we could be in God's kingdom when we function as one unit.

We have all the components to function but many are inoperable and isolated by habitual practices and mindsets that thwart our progress toward greatness and morph our identity from who we should be into what we have become, different versions of restrictive religious groups.

The kingdom in motion manifests when the creation connects with its Creator to rediscover its true identity and function with purpose.

According the Dr. Myles Munroe, *"It is most important to note that God the Creator chose the concept of a kingdom to communicate His purpose, will and plan for mankind and earth to us."* *"The kingdom was born in the heart of man, placed there by his Creator as the purpose for which he was created."* [2]

Similar to our DNA, (genetic makeup) we all have a blueprint inside of us that only the Creator knows. It is through God's instructions that humans understand what they were created to do. *"He has filled them with skill to do all kinds of work...all of them skilled workers and designers"* (Exodus 35:35). We are all fully equipped with the tools but there must be a connection in order to know how to use the tools, gifts and skillsets we are endowed with.

When you know your function the kingdom in you becomes visible to the world (as you let your light shine) through the direction of the Spirit of the Creator connecting with your spirit. But how do you know if you have his spirit? *"I will put my spirit within you, and cause you to walk in my statutes, and ye shall keep my judgement and do them"* (see Ezekiel 36:27 KJV).

DYNAMIC PARTICIPANTS

If you have his spirit you are his child, and if you are his child he wants you to prosper far beyond what you could see. He guides his children through all things.

Similar to a pilot in the dark night sky, you have no idea where you are going in life unless connected to the air traffic control tower. The pilot's only means of making it to safe landing is through the connection with air traffic control. Still, there are no guarantees and even though connected, this does not exempt the flight from turbulence or poor visibility due to bad weather, but the pilot stands a much greater chance of making it home if he stays connected and follows the instructions of the air traffic controller. If failure occurs in the connection between the pilot and the tower, it means zero direction, and no directions (in a night sky with hundreds of other planes) could mean chaos and imminent disaster.

The same concept above applies to every human being. We could be that plane in the dark night sky that has lost connection with the tower and continues to hover aimlessly until we are near the end of our fuel. Many of us are flying without a flight plan and only God himself knows the way we take.

The results could be frightening, but this does not have to be the case for you. Make the connection and stay connected so you can do more than just have a safe landing, but also enjoy your flight as you function with purpose. For this to happen there must be a connection to the source in order to receive the instructions for your life.

One of the principles in the kingdom is that God will give you instructions for what you were created to do. Through the work of the Holy Spirit he produces the things you desire as a function for his divine purpose. The second principle is that you are not void of struggles just because you are in the kingdom.

In the words of renowned singer, Wintley Phipps, *"It is in the quiet crucible of our personal private sufferings that our noblest dreams are born and our greatest gifts are given, and often given in compensation for what we have been through."* [3]

WHY DO WE NEED THE KINGDOM?

Only in the kingdom can you be the best original of what you were created to be; otherwise, you would be inclined to copy someone else or just be a shadow of what you could become. Without the kingdom, there is no order to existence, no purpose to living and no meaning to life. The true purpose for the gifts would remain hidden, your potential unreleased and motion without focus leads to chaos and self-destruction.

Without the kingdom you are just like that plane without a flight plan, disconnected from air traffic control, hovering somewhere in the dark night sky and about to run out of fuel.

Then again, you may have a blueprint but lack the wisdom to decode its purpose. You may have a map but do not have a clue about its destination, or how long it takes to get there. You may have data but without specific information, you will have no understanding of how to work the plan for your life. You may have wealth and riches but have no idea how to use it to transform the world for good.

The parable of the Prodigal Son is a great example of someone who had all the abundance of living but lacked the connection to access the provisions of his father. It was only after coming to his senses that the Prodigal Son reconnected with his father in a way that gave him access to his true wealth, (Luke 15: 11-32).

The kingdom has everything that pertains to life and fulfilment of the human spirit. You don't need religion; you need a relationship with your Creator. All this is found in the kingdom of God. It provides a blueprint for your life, a compass that guides and refocuses your vision for living abundantly.

Like the prodigal son, you no longer have to wander through life just hoping for something to happen, or settle for less than you are worth. You can be the change that makes a difference to transform your community and even the world. But sometimes we are closer than we think and still miss out.

WHERE WE MISS IT

What are the missing pieces that hinder the completion of the kingdom in motion in our lives? As humans we miss the kingdom when we overlook people for the practice of a religion. Most religions, even Christianity, miss the message for the messenger and the Christ for the "man" Jesus. As a mindset, we miss the kingdom when we value the container above its content.

Jesus, the *"earth-man"* is the container, but the message of *"Christ"* is what brings the transformation. It is *"Christ in you, the hope of glory"* (Colossians 1:27), that makes all the difference in us. If we miss the message of Christ, the teacher and counselor, we will only be different people but incapable of making a difference.

As a nation we miss the kingdom when we put policies ahead of cultivating caring communities. As industries of innovation and technology, we miss the kingdom when we praise the practitioner (the creation) but are reluctant to acknowledge where the ability comes from, the Creator.

As parents we miss the kingdom when we ignore and discourage our children instead of valuing and developing the gifts that are trapped inside of them.

As educators we miss the kingdom when we teach only for high scores and miss the opportunity to really help students to learn even the most basic concepts: to be creative, think critically, solve problems and communicate clearly.

But the good news is that no one is perfect; we are all striving for *perfection* and with the aid of *correction*, we can bridge the gap to making the right *connection*. As a side note: it is important for you to understand that *perfect* does not imply *perfection*; it simply means to *mature*, and *maturity* comes from growing every day as you are led by the Spirit of God.

Another function of the kingdom is to encourage each person to be the iron that sharpens the next iron so that we can all cut through confusion with clarity. You can be the change that empowers your community and the world. You and I are royalty designed to function as citizens in God's kingdom. Our next move then, is to take a good look into our spiritual mirrors and ponder if what we see is the reflection we want to live. If not, then what will you do about it?

WHAT DO YOU REFLECT?

I believe that one of the greatest inventions of all time is the mirror. Although it is only a piece of glass, it reflects what it sees and if you look careful enough you'll come to agree with the mirror. I do not write to convert you to any church or religion or make you feel guilty about your past choices (for Lord knows we have all messed up and fell extremely short of reflecting God's glory).

But sometimes our identities become tainted and we lose our way in life. We simply forget who we are and wander off to the nearest jungle of anesthesia that we hope will *"Hakuna Matata"* our pain away. But I'm reminded of a great story about a king who lost his sense of self and wandered off to an *anesthetic jungle* hoping to forget his past but was confronted with a mirror which reflected his true identity. The mirror requires our full attention and we must look long enough to truly discover what we seek.

The story of that young king was illustrated through an animated movie, The *Lion King*. In brief, Simba, the young king tried to run away from his past but was lured by his guide Rafiki, to a watering hole (a mirror) so Simba could see a reflection of the king inside of him. (See my other book, *Work Your Words: Finding Your Pathway to Personal Success*…"*The king inside of me"*). Many times we singlehandedly go through struggles when all we needed is a *Rafiki,* a real guide to lure us back to a watering hole so we can be reconnected to our true selves and reflect the kingdom inside of us. Why not start today?

EXCHANGING RELIGION FOR A LIFE OF FUNCTION AND PURPOSE

The purpose here is to get you to understand that who you are is far more than what you see. Seeing may be a function of the anatomical senses but looking is a skill which requires diligence and the focus to execute. What are you reflecting? Are you reflecting the king inside of you? And is the kingdom at work in you?

In order to reflect something you must be in the environment that reflects what it sees. But before you can see what to look for you must first know who you are. Your identity is found in your Creator. Anything less is simply a fake *Rembrandt* or a fictitious *Picasso*. As you make the kingdom your first priority, you will not only find yourself, you'll find the blueprint that helps you make sense of the reason you were created and answers to the many questions you might have.

For example:

Your *whys* may be: why me…?
Your *whats* may be: what am I supposed to do…?
Your *hows* may be: how am I supposed to do it…?
Your *Whens* may be: when is this supposed to happen…?
Your *Wheres* may be: where is the path I should take…?

I am excited for you! Let this be the day when your pursuit ends and your discovery to greatness begins. It has been a great journey sharing with you and I hope to have begun the conversation that will make the kingdom a more practical experience for everyone. I also hope that you are now more knowledgeable about yourself and our amazing Creator.

NOTES

Chapter 14: Dynamic Participants

1. Einstein, Albert. (DOCUMENTRY) Perf. Albert Einstein. *History Channel,History.com.*Https://www.youtube.com/watch?v=N0x9gApvuGo. Web. 01 Aug. 15.

2. Munroe, Myles. *Rediscovering the Kingdom: Ancient Hope for Our 21st Century World.* Shippensburg, PA: Destiny Image, 2004. (P 63, 64).

3. Phipps, Wintley. *Inspirational Speaker Motivational Speech. Wintley Phipps Online.*
https://www.youtube.com/watch?v=EcYnfgbEBh0
20 Jan. 2016. Web. 16 Apr. 2016.

EPILOGUE

"WE ARE ONE"

As we come to the end of our journey through these pages, (and I encourage you to read it again and share with others) I could only hope it was time well spent. I trust that you were encouraged, motivated, inspired and challenged on many instances regarding your faith, your life, your purpose, your function and the role you play as an organ in the body and in the big picture of creation. In the end, if there was *"ONE"* take-away I would like you to have from reading this book it is this: *WE Have ONE Creator!*

And while we may look different, there are so many other traits and characteristics that make us even more similar than we are willing to admit. Under the canopy of the vast sky, we are the same—*HUMANITY*. We have what I call *ACTOOO: atoms* that make up cells, *cells* that make up tissues, *tissues* that make up organs, *organs* that make up organ-systems, and a complex *organ-system* that makes each of us a living *organism*. In short, you get the acronym (ACTOOO), which means interdependently connected. Out of one (God) we became many members, but one people with many functions for one purpose—to create a presence on earth that is a reflection of God's kingdom in motion.

True enough, and according to the world, we are divided by our beliefs, customs, external appearances and characteristics, but at the spiritual and biological core of creation the same gift of life flows through our bodies—blood. And while we may have different beginnings and diverse experiences, we are all part of the grand circle of life. This circle is the culmination and the sum total of our uniqueness that make us one. In a body of many parts with diverse functions and specialized gifts, it is the utilization of our functional gifts in specific communities which makes life possible and living worth pursuing. *I need you to be you so I can be me.* We complete each other. When you function, I benefit and the world becomes a better place. No one lives to himself or herself alone; neither can the body survive without the heart, the brain, lung nor any of its parts, which makes the body one complete organism.

DIFFERENT YET THE SAME

The message of this book is clear: in the kingdom of God, WE ARE ONE! No one person is superior to the other. No part of the human body is *vestigial* (functionless or imperceptible) or

EPILOGUE: THE ANATOMY OF THE KINGDOM

more special than the other—not the heart of the circulatory system, neither the lung of the respiratory system, the muscles and bones of the moving parts, nor the brain and its thinking parts. Every part plays a role. Moreover, even though some scientists (who have not lived long enough to know it all) say otherwise, I submit that no part of the body is *vestigial* in function or purpose. No human has uncovered the body in its totality to suggest otherwise.

Even in our greatest achievements of science and technology, and human ingenuity, we've only barely scratched the surface of our complexity. We are differently the same. *This difference makes us special enough to be honored for the function we do in our area of giftedness.*

The body honors the heart for its function and service in the community of the circulatory system; likewise, the nervous system honors the brain as it innervates the body to transmit crucial information to its neighboring counterparts. Breathing is the body's way of honoring the lung for its function and service in the community of the respiratory system.

Without lungs, oxygen would be *used-less* and the body would cease to live. Although they are difference, each contribution makes life possible. *So are we in the kingdom—differently the same!*

Think of it this way; God is superior and above all, but he demonstrates his function of *"ONE PURPOSE"* through the Holy Spirit living inside of us to transform the world. For this reason you are God's power in the earth realm; his hands and feet, eyes and voice/mouthpiece. You are more powerful than you think, because you have God on the inside. Your purpose

THE ANATOMY OF THE KINGDOM

and function make you a great asset to society, a key component in the body of your community (where you live, work, play and pray), and a reflection of *the kingdom of God in motion!*

TAKE ANOTHER LOOK AT THE QUESTION BELOW:

If the world were an interconnected body made up of diverse organs, which organ would you be and what would be your function?

WE'VE STARTED THE CONVERSATION. NOW LET'S BEGIN THE PROCESS TO FUNCTION WITH PURPOSE.

PRAYER OF LIBERATION IS
A GREAT PLACE TO BEGIN.
(SEE NEXT PAGE).

KINGDOM PRAYER OF LIBERATION
"The Anatomy of the Kingdom"
[By: Andrew E. Guy]

#1 My God, my creator,
#2 My life is in your hands.
#3 I invite you into my circumstance to awaken your treasure that is buried in me.
#4 Take all my plans, aspirations and desires and direct my steps to a path that glorifies you.
#5 Let no sin rule over me and redeem me from the clutches of human oppression.
#6 Create in me a heart of service that I may use my gifts and talents to serve people, your image in the earth.
#7 Let me function with Excellency based on your original blueprint design.
#8 Help me to understand your purpose that my soul may know it and that I may see myself as you see me, fearfully and wonderfully crafted.
#9 As a member of the body, I could be a cell among trillions, a tissue among billions, an organ among millions, a system among thousands, hundreds, and even tens, but you made us one.
#10 I am ready to begin a functional journey that is free of human limitations.
#11 Use me that I may be a light to the dark, and a salt that preserves your creation, for in this you are glorified.
#12 Amen!

```
┌─────────────────────────────────────────────┐
│   GET THE MOST VALUE FROM THIS BOOK         │
│          "JOIN THE EMAIL LIST"              │
│         Sign up to receive                  │
│      "POWER OF COMMUNITY"                   │
│          Every Week!                        │
└─────────────────────────────────────────────┘
```

The Power of Community is a free monthly e-mail from Andrew E. Guy. This short message brings you powerful, inspirational and personal growth tools to help you transform your life in these areas: family, faith, community.

You are encouraged to share this information with as many people as you can. *My motto is:* if you care you'll share.

Sign up for "Power of Community" at
www.andrewguyspeaks.com

"...because great things happens when we connect"
~Andrew E. Guy

> # Staff Training & Development Bring:
> # "The POWER OF COMMUNITY"
> ## To your company/organization!

Bring **The Power of Community**™ seminar/workshop to your organization. This power training focuses on building communities in your company to boost productivity, improve communication and people skills through effective leadership development.

AREA OF FOCUS AND WHAT YOU'LL LEARN:
[*Faith . Athletics . Corporate . Education*]

- Leaders Are Spiritual Athletes: How Activate The Winning S.P.I.R.IT of the Athletic Leader
- How to make your team **M.I.T.E** ™
- How to build community and what makes it work
- The role of diversity in productivity
- How to effectively communicate what you want
- How to lead without being the boss
- How to identity the right people to build a team
- Understanding the framework of human needs

To request this training for your organization
Please visit: **Andrewguyspeaks.com**

BOOKS & RESOURCES:
Inquire about bulk orders for your staff:

ORDER YOUR COPY TODAY

Contact Us.
Glad share Media Publishing
info@gladsharemedia.com
www.gladsharemedia.com

OTHER BOOKS BY THE AUTHOR:

WORK YOUR WORDS: FINDING YOUR PATHWAY TO PERSONAL SUCCESS: If there was ever a book with easy-to-understand steps and built-in core values that tug at your heart and push you to take action, it's this one. Discover how to build courage, dream bigger, live label-free, and find your area of "giftedness" to change your life now.

Both failure and success are products of the mind; therefore, your limitations exist only by the way you think, and your world is created through the words you speak. Changing your thinking changes your words, and "right-speaking" changes your way of living. "YOU" have the power to change "YOUR LIFE." No more excuses!

> **"YOUR CALL TO ACTION"**
> *Let's start the conversation today. Share this book with your church, organization, business leadership team: Text a friend or Tweet your favorite quotes and post it on Social-Media.*
>
> FOLLOW ANDREW:
> **Twitter.com**/andrewguyspeaks
> **Linkedin.com**/in/andrewguyspeaks.

GET UPDATES: UPCOMING BOOK TOUR
JOIN THE MAILING LIST

****

I AM LOOKING FORWARD TO CONNECTING WITH YOU!

www.ingramcontent.com/pod-product-compliance
Lightning Source LLC
Chambersburg PA
CBHW021808220426
43662CB00006B/226